GETTING YOUR SHARE OF THE PIE

The Complete Guide to Finding Grants

VALERIE J. MANN

 PRAEGER

AN IMPRINT OF ABC-CLIO, LLC

Santa Barbara, California • Denver, Colorado • Oxford, England

Library of Congress Cataloging-in-Publication Data

Mann, Valerie J.
　Getting your share of the pie : the complete guide to finding
grants / Valerie J. Mann.
　　　p. cm.
　　Includes index.
　　ISBN 978-0-313-38254-3 (hard copy : alk. paper) — ISBN 978-0-313-38255-0
(ebook)
　　1. Fund raising.　2. Grants-in-aid.　3. Proposal writing for grants.　I. Title.
　　HG177.M36　2010
　　658.15'224—dc22　　　　2010015957

ISBN: 978-0-313-38254-3
EISBN: 978-0-313-38255-0

14　13　12　11　10　　1　2　3　4　5

This book is also available on the World Wide Web as an eBook.
Visit www.abc-clio.com for details.

Praeger
An Imprint of ABC-CLIO, LLC

ABC-CLIO, LLC
130 Cremona Drive, P.O. Box 1911
Santa Barbara, California 93116-1911

This book is printed on acid-free paper ∞

Manufactured in the United States of America

Dedicated with love, admiration, and respect to my son,
Brett Mann,
who has provided support, advice, and help beyond measure

Contents

Preface

It seems that as I go about my travels, I hear more and more people say excitedly, "I would love to learn how to write grants!" Grant writing is a field that increasingly fascinates people. Numerous times I have been conversing with someone about another topic when, upon finding out that I am a grant writer, they immediately want to talk about that instead. Maybe it is the appeal of finding money that is a "gift," or maybe it is the excitement of seeing a project that was once an idea on paper coming to full fruition.

In any event, there seems to be a big mystique about grant writing. Many people that I have talked to seem to feel that it is a profession that is so fraught with complexities and difficulties that only a very few can learn how to do it. These people seem to feel that it is not something to which they can aspire. They tend to look upon it as a major struggle and could not realistically conceive of writing a successful grant application.

I have been a successful grant writer for over 32 years. During that time, I estimate conservatively that I have written over 900 grant applications. Over 80 percent of these have been successful, with a yield to my clients of approximately $95,000,000. These clients are primarily cities, towns, counties, fire departments, police departments, and nonprofit organizations.

Grant writing expertise is very much in demand. Most of the larger governmental entities and nonprofits are able to afford full-time grant writers. The smaller entities that cannot afford grant writing staff generally miss out on grant monies. Ironically, it is the organizations that cannot afford grant writers who need grant funds the most. The significant demand for my services shows that the staff in many small towns and nonprofits does not have the expertise to obtain grant funds. In many cases, they are stretched so thin that even if they had some knowledge of the field, it would be impossible for them to spend substantial amounts of time on grant searches and grant writing.

The funding process for the American Recovery and Reinvestment Act (ARRA) of 2009 is a very good example of the demand that exists for experienced grant writers. I will refer specifically to one particular piece of this legislation that has provided funding for law enforcement through a number of major federal programs. The individual states have also received some of these funds to pass through to the local law enforcement agencies. However, this pass-through is not automatic. The agencies still must submit an application. I have heard it said time and time again that many of the small police departments are totally missing an opportunity to obtain some of these funds for much-needed equipment, new personnel, and overtime. I consistently hear comments like, "I know there is a lot of money out there for us, but we just don't know how to get it." Most of these agencies are so busy providing law enforcement services that they do not have the funds or the personnel to pursue grants that could make their job easier. This seems to be a vicious cycle.

There is thus a significant demand for additional grant writers who can also undertake searches for funding. However, there appears to be a shortage of training resources. This book is written with an eye toward filling this need. It can be used as a stand-alone resource or as a textbook for college level courses. Once the reader finishes, she should be able to immediately access grant search resources and begin to look for funds.

This book is a complete guide to every step of the process and will be especially useful to the novice. It is packed with information for anyone who wants to obtain more grant money for their organization or for those who wish to enter the grant writing field on either a consulting basis or as staff. The reader will be fully equipped with all the information necessary to be a success in this field. The book will demonstrate how the grant writer must think critically from the identification of the need to project design to grant searches all the way to the writing of the grant applications. Specific sources for undertaking a complete grant search will be identified.

The reader will also learn how to write grant proposals that stand the best chance of being funded. A multitude of grant writing tips are offered. Obtaining grants is a highly specialized and competitive field, and this book will give the aspiring grant writer the background information necessary in order to know how federal, state, and private funds are awarded.

Some of the useful features of this book are as follows:

- It will take the mystique out of grant writing and let the reader know that learning this profession is achievable and rewarding.

- Historical and current information regarding the general availability of government and private grant funds is offered.
- Specific places to search for grant funds for a particular type of project are given.
- The importance of developing a sound project that will fill the identified need will be discussed in detail.
- Information will be given on how to make inquiries of the various potential funding sources once they have been identified and how to develop a winning strategy.
- Writing suggestions and hints are prominently featured.
- The book will be a vehicle by which local governments and non-profits can train their staff to identify grant sources and obtain grant funds.

Included is a list of specific Web sites and print resources that the reader can use to actually begin searching for grant funds. This listing shows which sources are free of charge and which can be obtained only for a fee. Also included are examples of well-written grant proposals, budgets, and letters of inquiry as well as an exhaustive list of "dos" and "don'ts" culled from my many conversations with government and private funding sources over the years.

It has been my goal to make this information as clear and simple as possible in order to demystify the grant process. In my opinion, the grant writer follows a process that is actually quite simple and follows intuitive thinking. A good example of this is identifying the need that exists and developing a project that will not only fill that need, but that is fundable. From there, the grant writer will look at the many search resources available to identify sources of funding and begin to develop a plan for obtaining the funds. This book will help by having this information all in one place and serving as a reference guide that can be referred to time and time again. Of course, as in any other profession, one gets better with experience. Learning is greatly enhanced by taking the things learned from a guidebook and doing it oneself.

There are certain subtle nuances of judgment that can only be learned by having to make these types of judgment calls over a long period of time. It is certain that reading this book will not immediately make one an expert in the field of grant writing. However, it will equip the reader with the tools needed to get started.

Those who wish to receive further training in grant writing and administration should attend the two-day seminars I give throughout the country. These seminars cover all of the material in this book but have the advantage of providing a student with the opportunity to interact with me on a live basis. In addition, the presence of other class members can make the material more meaningful, as class discussions can often bring out nuances that would not be immediately evident in the book. The schedule and registration information for these seminars is given on my Web site, http://www.gettingyour shareofthepie.com. The Foundation Center and the Grantsmanship Center also give seminars in selected cities throughout the country. I urge the grant seeker to take advantage of any classes or seminars offered by state or federal funding agencies. For the most part, these will be specific to a particular program and are generally free of charge.

It is also important to remember that one's success rates can vary from time to time for many reasons. I would therefore caution the reader to not become discouraged by several rejections. This may mean that the project should be redesigned, or it may mean that there is a greater need associated with other projects in the competition. I have seen many projects receive funding on the second or even third try.

This is a very rewarding field in which to work, and I feel privileged to be able to share this information with the reader. I have enjoyed being a grant writer for several reasons. One of the most important is the fact that it is a real thrill to receive those award letters. Following that, seeing the actual project evolve with the use of grant funds makes a grant writer feel that he is making a real difference. Seeing a police department, for example, receive the funds to hire additional officers and provide a heightened level of patrol in a crime-ridden neighborhood is just one example of helping to make the world a better place. The citizens in those neighborhoods will feel more safe and secure, and their quality of life will be vastly improved. Another example is seeing a significant historic building in ruins and in danger of deteriorating completely brought back to its former grandeur with funds from heritage tourism programs.

Being in this field has enabled me to have the privilege of working with many different types of projects, all of which have their own rewards. I have obtained funds for clients in the following fields: law enforcement, housing rehabilitation, water and sewer service, street work and storm drainage, economic development, downtown revitalization, recreation and parks, the fire service, historic preservation, and heritage tourism. It has truly been a pleasure to have been involved in the enhancement of life that these projects have provided. It is my sincere wish that the reader will take the information contained in this book and use it for the betterment of their community and the world at large.

It is my great pleasure to acknowledge the wonderful assistance and support I have gotten from a number of sources. These people have certainly made my task easier and have enabled me to sail through the process, which is the way it should be. Writing and publishing a book such as this is the capstone of one's career and should be enjoyed and savored to the fullest extent.

First and foremost, I would like to acknowledge my wonderful and talented son and business partner, Brett Mann. He willingly assisted with the small amount of research that was necessary for this book. In addition, he worked with me closely in editing and in last-minute fact checking. His perspective has brought fresh ideas to our work, and this is reflected in the book. Sometimes it is necessary to sit back and benefit from the unbiased opinions of others. One of his most valuable talents is to be able to look at a situation and immediately identify both the problems and the strong points. His quick, keen, highly analytical mind and common sense approach has been a real asset to the business. Brett is a master at solving problems in a no-nonsense, "let's get to the heart of the issue" manner. His ability to think outside of the box will stand him in good stead in any situation.

I would also like to thank and acknowledge my many clients over the years. This book would not have been possible without the experience that they have provided to me. I have been very fortunate to have worked with some very knowledgeable and talented individuals who truly have the best interests of their organizations at heart. I look at many of these people as my partners in working for the betterment of their environment. As the grant applications are approved and the funds come in, I feel the same sense of happiness and pride as they do. Many of them have retained my services to implement the project and administer the grant. This gives me the pleasure of seeing the project through to completion. It is a wonderful feeling to see the benefits that accrue to individuals and organizations as a whole. This is the best part of the job.

It has been a great pleasure to work with Praeger to produce this book. The company is top-notch, and everyone I have dealt with has been a consummate professional. Jeff Olson was the editor to whom I originally submitted the manuscript. His support of the idea from the very beginning kept me encouraged throughout the evaluation process. Even though I am sure that he was extremely busy and was working with a number of other authors, he always had time to respond promptly to my questions. I wish him the very best in his new enterprise, as he left the company in November of 2009. His successor, Brian Romer, is just as professional and responsive. His steady hand and patience throughout the process have helped us to produce a book of which I am justly proud. Even though the staff is responsible for a large number of titles each year, I have never felt as if I am just one author out of many. Praeger has a wonderful talent for making one feel unique and important.

Chapter One

Overview and General Information

MY TAKE ON THE GRANT WORLD TODAY

Why this book? Why now? It would seem that grant seeking and grant writing would always be of great interest. After all, everyone likes to find ways to get money for their pet projects, right? This is only human nature.

However, in the 32 years that I have been writing grant applications, I have never seen the level of interest that I am seeing now. It is beyond the scope of this book to speculate as to why. My best guess is that the state of the economy and the economic stimulus package provided by the American Recovery and Reinvestment Act (ARRA) of 2009, which pumped an extensive amount of grant money into the economy, has played some role.

Being a well-rounded person, I have other interests besides my work. I am very interested in outdoor activities and get to as many beaches and state and federal parks as I can. I find this a very relaxing antidote to the sometimes stressful world of grant deadlines. Just when I think I am spending my leisure time away from the grant world, I am approached by someone about doing some grant work for their organization. Just as an accountant is always asked to be the treasurer of whatever group they belong to, I find myself looking for grants for organizations connected with my outside interests.

I can be traveling and encounter a stranger who, when he or she hears what I do, is deeply interested and always seems to know a person or organization that needs assistance in grant writing. I can be sitting in a restaurant and be talking about work with my companion and have other people in the vicinity approach me and want to talk about grant seeking.

In any event, that is the major reason I am writing this book. There seems to be a major fascination with finding grant funds. Perhaps it is the prestige that comes with being a "rainmaker" (one who brings money into the organization). Perhaps it is the satisfaction that comes with seeing a need, maybe even an urgent need, and following the process all the way through to implementing the project.

This book will give you the tools to begin a full-time or part-time career in the grant field. Or perhaps you would rather just work as a volunteer for your favorite organization. In any event, I am writing this to let you know where to go to find the money and how to get it once you have found potential sources.

I graduated from American University in Washington, D.C., with a B.A. in Foreign Policy Analysis in 1973. Upon graduation from college, I worked in the office of a restaurant chain in Ocean City, Maryland, and then in the Public Information Office at the Federal Reserve Board in Washington, D.C. I was not aware that there were any classes in grant writing on the college level at that time.

In July 1977, I was lucky enough to get a job writing grant applications in the Mayor's Office of the City of Salisbury, Maryland. I had no experience with grants at the time. Salisbury, with a population of about 24,000 people, is the regional hub of the Delmarva Peninsula, located between the Atlantic Ocean and the Chesapeake Bay. The peninsula contains parts of Delaware, Maryland, and Virginia, as its name implies. Salisbury is the cultural, business, health care, shopping, and governmental center for this 14-county region.

My new job was a "learn as you go" experience. No one else in the city government worked full time in the grants field. My boss, the Executive Secretary (or City Administrator as the position is known today), had a number of other duties besides supervising me. The major funding program with which the city was involved was the Community Development Block Grant Program (CDBG). At that time, the program was administered by the U.S. Department of Housing and Urban Development (HUD). It still exists to this day and is relatively unchanged from that time. However, the individual states have taken on the administration of this program, but they must operate under HUD's supervision. This program is extremely popular among municipalities and counties due to the fact that significant amounts of money can be garnered, and the funds can be used for a wide range of activities.

After six years in that job, I worked for a nonprofit for a couple of years, further honing and refining my grant writing skills. I felt that working in that environment would round out my training.

I then began to have grandiose ideas about being a grant consultant. Even then, I wondered whether I had enough experience to really bill myself as an expert in this field. However, my solution in life has been to forge ahead regardless of doubts.

Fortunately, an opportunity appeared for a one-year consulting contract with the Coastal Counties Community Housing Resources Board for

Wicomico and Somerset Counties in Maryland. This contract would keep me busy for approximately three days a week on projects related to the fair housing laws, which state that there will be no discrimination in the housing market. The consultant fees were to be paid with grant funds awarded by HUD. The job included the writing of a landlord–tenant manual, giving talks to elderly and disadvantaged groups regarding their rights under the fair housing laws, organizing a fair housing poster contest, and arranging for municipalities in the area to issue fair housing month proclamations. The fee was only a little less than my salary in the full-time job.

About six months after that, I picked up a second consulting job. This was for the Worcester County government administering a housing rehabilitation program funded by a Community Development Block Grant. That was the beginning of a rewarding consulting career.

My business has thrived. It is almost as if all I had to do was just make the decision to go from being a full-time employee to becoming a "grant expert." I am giving this history so that the reader may know that much of the learning in grant work takes place on the job.

I am very fortunate to have a variety of clients, and I have worked with a wide array of federal, state, and private funding agencies. The following federal funding agencies and offices have provided grant monies to my clients for numerous projects: National Park Service, Economic Development Administration of the U.S. Department of Commerce, the U.S. Department of Housing and Urban Development, the U.S. Department of Justice, the Federal Emergency Management Agency, the U.S. Department of Agriculture, and the Environmental Protection Agency. In my home state of Maryland, I have been successful in obtaining grant funds for my clients from the Department of Natural Resources, the Department of the Environment, the Department of Housing and Community Development, the Maryland Heritage Areas Authority, and the Maryland Historical Trust. Several private and quasi-public entities have also provided funding for my projects. These have included the France-Merrick Foundation of Baltimore, Preservation Maryland, the National Trust for Historic Preservation, and the Fair Play Foundation of Wilmington, Delaware.

I have had some wonderful clients, most of whom I have served for many years. Naturally, a sense of camaraderie and a common purpose develops in working with the same clients year after year. I greatly value their contributions to the communities in which they operate.

SUCCESS VS. FAILURE

I would like to take this opportunity right at the very beginning of the book to say a few words about what constitutes *success*. In our all too competitive society, it sometimes seems as if we measure our success by the number of "competitors" we outdo. There is some truth to this in the grant writing field because there are often numerous applicants competing for what seems like a very small amount of money. The field can be inherently ego-deflating if a grant application is either denied or funded only in part. The measurement of our accomplishments is thus very concrete. It is not like some other jobs whose measurements of success are sometimes rather fuzzy.

I would like to interject some of my personal philosophy about being confident in the workplace. One should rest easy knowing that one has done the best that she can do and accept the occasional failure. I realize that this is easy for me to say from my perspective. The reader may very well say that I can afford to be confident because I have proven myself. The point that I am trying to make is that although much of the success or failure of a grant application depends upon the skill of a writer, it is by no means the only factor in the outcome.

Not being a very competitive sort, I used to dread going to the yearly opening meetings of a particular grant competition when I was working for the City of Salisbury from 1977 to 1985. Inevitably, the coffee breaks and lunch hours would be taken up with people nervously circulating around the room talking to one another about their latest funded project and how well they had done with it. This was a very competitive program, and everyone was very aware that we were competing with the other people in the room. However, underneath the very positive spin, there was a great deal of insecurity. It was as if we all wanted the others to know how many applications we had had funded so that we could establish our place in the pecking order of the group. I realize that it sounds impossible to accomplish, but I would strongly advise a prospective grant writer to not compare themselves to others.

If there is a really great project and the funding agency is aware of it and wants to fund it, they are generally more tolerant of minor flaws in the application. One example that I can think of is very telling. A small town was searching for funds for a street extension that would help to move traffic into and out of the downtown area more easily. The President of the Town Council, being very politically oriented and astute, was able to interest a state funding agency in this project based just on its merits. However, an application had to be filed. The Town's Manager/Clerk was accordingly asked to prepare the application. Years later, I heard that the funding agency thought it was the worst application they had ever seen. However, due to the merits of the project, it received funding.

Sometimes even the best applications are not successful. One example that illustrates this beautifully is a story I heard about a municipality who was applying to the state government for funds to rehabilitate a street that was in imminent danger of collapse. There was a very real need here, and the only solution was a costly ($400,000) complete rehabilitation of the street. This town had a population of only 750 people, and only about 50 residents on the street would benefit most directly. The application was turned down the first year it was submitted. The funding agency was good enough to make a regular practice of letting the applicants who did not get funded know the reason for that decision. In that case, they mentioned a few minor issues with the narrative, which were easily corrected. However, their main problem seemed to be centered on the fact that no other funding sources were being sought. It was obvious that they did not feel comfortable making a grant of that size and being the only funding agency involved in the project.

Unfortunately, grant sources for municipal street work are not plentiful in that part of the country. The town reapplied the next year and made the requested narrative changes. An attempt was made to find other sources to leverage, or match, the state monies. The town was able to show that it had at least tried to find other funds. However, the town itself, with its budget of only $375,000 per year, could not afford to put any money into it. The application was turned down for the second time even though the town did everything that the state asked for with the exception of contributing its own money to the project. This was a very unfortunate case because the project really needed to be done, and there was no other place to turn. However, this just goes to show that the best written project can be turned down because of situations beyond the grant writer's control.

I have sometimes had to tell clients that their idea for a particular project was not very fundable. Or, I have had to tell them that a particular program did not seem to be a good match and that they would probably not receive the funds from that source. Knowing that, however, I have still had clients tell me to proceed based on the fact that a 20 percent chance was just that—a chance that would not be there if they did not apply. Clearly, in those cases, I did not feel like a failure if the application was not funded. I can see their logic, as long as the odds are not too long. For example, a yacht club that wishes to receive grant money for a membership drive should understand that this project will rank much lower than those that address basic living needs of low- and moderate-income people.

WHAT I HOPE THIS BOOK WILL ACCOMPLISH

My purpose in writing this book is to disseminate a complete "how to" guide to the grant world. The reference component of the book will give the reader additional resources to consult as their grant writing career proceeds. This will ensure that the serious student is given the tools to keep up with the most current information in the field. I will begin with the most basic element of receiving a grant—identifying the true need—and conclude with steps to be taken if the grant application is not approved. In the pages in between, I will guide the reader on how to develop a fundable project, find the most promising grant sources, develop a strategy for which sources to approach, and write a successful proposal.

However, as in my own experience, time spent on the job is critically important. There are, as in any other profession, various nuances and subtleties that show themselves as one actually begins to work. No book can cover all of those situations. We all know how various judgment points are different at different parts of one's career. The seasoned veteran will obviously think of the proper questions to ask and look behind the scenes to see what is not obvious, whereas a novice might tend to take the situation at face value.

One example of how experience is just as important as knowledge is my policy of looking for "deal breakers" in the very beginning of an assignment. I examine the project closely and consult the funding agency if there is any doubt as to project eligibility. This may sound like common sense, but the novice has a tendency to want to think that the project is fundable under a particular program regardless of any issues that may be a potential problem. He may not want to think that this potential source, which may have been very hard to find, may not be the right choice. I highly recommend that the grant writer minutely examine the program guidelines at least twice in order to ensure that the project is eligible for funding.

I was once hired to write a grant application for a nonprofit agency whose director assured me that his marketing project was eligible for a program administered by the U.S. Department of Commerce. He explained that he had attended a meeting at which he was told that the project had a high likelihood of getting funded. However, after reading the guidelines, I had a nagging suspicion that all was not well. Accordingly, I contacted the agency, who informed me that there had been a misunderstanding and that this project would not even meet their threshold requirements—meaning that it would not even be reviewed. "Threshold" refers to the minimum criteria to even be eligible to apply. Going the extra mile to check saved both me and the nonprofit from a potentially embarrassing and expensive mistake.

Another very obvious skill that the aspiring grant writer can only pick up with experience is making contacts within the various funding agencies. In my case, this has been carefully developed over the years. I am proud to say that the funding agencies I work with know me as an individual who lives up to her promises, meets deadlines without exception, and understands the restrictions under which that agency is working. I would advise the novice grant writer to deal with funding agencies with the utmost honesty. One of the worst things anyone can do is leave the impression that you are trying to "pull the wool over their eyes." Most of the agencies can pick this up in a heartbeat. Needless to say, this leaves a very bad impression of the grant writer that can linger for years.

The following are the skills that I hope this book will instill in budding grant writers:

- The ability to think critically of the "big picture" when crafting projects
- Recognition that ill-conceived projects very rarely get funded
- Basic knowledge of the types of funding agencies
- The ability to speak "grant language"
- Basic knowledge of grant search resources and the ability to know how to check for updates
- Development of a writing style that is clear, simple, direct, and to the point
- Development of oral communications skills, which will be helpful in dealing with the funding agencies
- Development of the ability to administer a grant properly
- Basic knowledge of research techniques
- Knowledge of basic ethical principles

This book will not accomplish the following:

- It will not be a substitute for your own common sense—this book cannot cover every conceivable situation.
- It will not be a complete and advanced writing course—general writing principles will be covered briefly prior to the more detailed information regarding writing a grant proposal.
- It will not prepare you for some of the quirky little things that happen in the grant writing field—after all of these years, I still get surprised occasionally.

EVERYTHING MUST BE DONE IN A LOGICAL SEQUENCE

I have already implied this several times and will most definitely repeat it throughout the book, but there is a very significant element of grant writing that is just plain common sense. This involves seeing the logic of the process from beginning to end. Naturally, the way a proposal is written will have a large impact on whether it is funded or not. However, before we get to the writing, there is the research involved in finding the right sources. Prior to that, and most importantly, is the identification of the need and the project design. These are the building blocks of the grant writer's quest to receive funds.

In my experience, it is more important to have a good project than it is to have a perfectly written grant proposal. If a project is poorly conceived, will not fit the need, or the need is fuzzy, a professional writing job can only accomplish so much. Naturally, the writer wants to bring out the best points of any project. A good grant writer can extract and elaborate on the elements of a project that fit the funding guidelines. However, most agencies and foundations are savvy enough to see through this. They are looking more for a good project that will help to fulfill their aims, objectives, and funding priorities. Most federal and state funding agencies are under strict guidelines in giving out grant funds. Many programs have specific rating and ranking criteria with points assigned to each rating factor. They do not have much room for discretion and must adhere to their regulations.

This is why it is so important to pay even more attention in the beginning when the need is being identified. This first step is the foundation for the entire process. If the grant seeker does not correctly identify a specific need, the rest of the process will be flawed, for obvious reasons.

I would like to tell the reader an anecdote that illustrates the importance of learning each step in its proper order. I once took a graduate-level statistics class and was fortunate enough to receive an "A." The class was quite difficult, however, and although I have been a good student throughout my life, I had to spend a great deal of time reading and re-reading the material in order to make sure that I understood the concepts. It soon became apparent that unless the student mastered each step in logical order, it was completely impossible to understand the next step. For example, if Chapter 2 was not thoroughly mastered and completely understood, it was impossible to even begin to understand Chapter 3. The student could become hopelessly lost in no time.

The same principle is at work in the grant-seeking process. If the need is not correctly identified, then any project that is devised to fill this incorrect need is not going to be credible. If the project is not credible, the proposal will be a poor one, despite the best efforts of the writer.

Much of this is obvious. However, I have seen many instances where applicants just wish to have a particular project funded regardless of whether it is needed or not. For example, an agency that wishes to acquire additional vehicles and equipment just because someone else has more will not stand much chance of getting funded. Despite the talk of wasteful spending at all levels of government, I have found that federal and state funding agencies, with their limited grant resources, are very adept at spotting requests for projects that waste funds.

TYPES OF ASSISTANCE—GRANTS, LOW-INTEREST LOANS, AND IN-KIND CONTRIBUTIONS

Most seekers of funds want to go after grants. This is the most common type of assistance, and as the name implies, grants do not need to be repaid. Although there are legal requirements on the spending of the money and various contractual obligations, grant funds are provided without any obligation for repayment. In some cases, however, there may be provisions for repayment if certain obligations are not met.

One example would be misuse of the funds, either through dishonesty or inattention to the provisions of the grant agreement. I am aware of several municipalities that were forced to repay a portion of their grant due to the fact that the money was not spent properly or certain required administrative steps were not taken. One relatively small city was awarded funds to help low- and moderate-income homeowners in a particular section of town hook up to the municipal water system. They were required to have any families wishing to receive this assistance fill out an application and document the fact that their income was below a certain level. This was required with the idea that the grant money would only pay for connections for families in lower income brackets and not just anyone in the neighborhood. However, the community skipped this essential process and just went ahead and connected everyone. As a result, they had to repay a hefty portion of the grant. I do not know to this day how they were able to find the money to do this.

Another example of certain cases where grant funds must be repaid is a requirement of the CDBG program that states any households receiving housing rehabilitation assistance must be willing to place a lien upon their home. In most cases, if the house is not sold within a period of five years, no repayment is required. However, if the house is sold within one year after the rehabilitation work is completed, they must repay 100 percent of the funds used to fix the house. If they sell the property within two years of the time the work is completed, they must repay 80 percent of the funds. The amount of the grant to be repaid goes down by 20 percent for each year that the house is still owned by the original owners.

In cases where municipalities receive funds for downtown improvement projects to assist individual businesses, the funding agency most often requires that this assistance be given in the form of a loan. The funds are made as a grant to the municipality, which in turn lends the money to businesses. The municipality may structure the program so that the interest rates are affordable and the terms easy. When repayments are received, in many cases, the municipality may keep the funds to loan to other businesses.

I have noted in recent years that certain state agencies are starting to use the term *reimbursable program*. This means that the grantee must pay the cost of the project up front and will then be reimbursed by the granting agency. To me this sounds like a grant program, although special arrangements must be made to find money somewhere, perhaps with a bank loan, to pay for the project before receiving reimbursement. However, in the final analysis, the funding agency will pay for the program. It is interesting to note that one federal agency using this methodology states specifically in the grant instructions that "This is not a grant program—this is a reimbursement program." However, the net effect is the same—the funding agency pays for the project.

Most seekers of funds would prefer to not have to repay a loan. However, sometimes this is the only alternative. Loan money may be the only source of funds available, or the applicant may not qualify for a grant. The U.S. Department of Agriculture's (USDA) Community Facilities Program provides both grant and loan funds. However, the amount of grant funds is limited to $50,000 for each particular project. For smaller projects, this may be adequate. However, for larger projects, USDA often offers a combination grant–loan deal. For example, the available sources to build new firehouses are very few and far between. The Community Facilities Program is one of the few that will fund this type of project. However, most building projects far exceed $50,000. Therefore, new firehouse projects receive most of the assistance in the form of a loan. The terms are very favorable, with the interest rate ranging between 4 percent and 5 percent for a 30- or 40-year term. This is a good way to finance the project when loan funds are the only alternative.

The Maryland Department of the Environment (MDE) offers very popular loan programs as well as grant programs. The agency also offers grant funds. Municipalities and counties within Maryland are the eligible applicants for the water and sewer programs offered by MDE. Most of them are struggling to provide affordable water and sewer service to their residents. In order to keep rates low, especially in communities where there are many persons on fixed incomes, it is not possible to amass significant amounts of money to undertake major repairs or expansions. The agency assesses whether the community can afford to repay a loan and will offer certain applicants grant funds, while other applicants will only be offered loans. However, the interest rate on loans in "disadvantaged communities" can often be less than 1 percent. MDE has specific guidelines for qualifying as a disadvantaged community.

I will occasionally receive inquiries from for-profit businesses. Much of the governmental money available for businesses is in the form of either a low-interest loan, loan guarantee (where the funding agency guarantees a bank loan and will repay this loan if the borrower defaults), or an equity investment in the company. An equity investment is an amount of funds given to the business in exchange for part ownership. There seems to be a general impression in the marketplace that the federal and state governments are offering tons and tons of grant money to help businesses and that they could get it if they only knew how to access it. This is, in general, not true, and I have had to tamp down the expectations of several businesses that have approached me. Two of the major agencies assisting businesses, the Small Business Administration and the U.S. Department of Agriculture, offer primarily loans and loan guarantees.

The popular CDBG program provides funding for economic development projects. This is the one source that I know will provide grant funds to assist in business development. Needless to say, there must be a significant public purpose to the project—in most cases, large numbers of new jobs must be created. Also, the grant funds usually represent a small percentage of the total cost. The more economically distressed the area is, the more likely it is that these funds will be granted.

One example that comes to mind is a shop that will be developed in conjunction with a transportation museum. Grant funds are being provided to construct an addition that will house this shop and provide a respectable number of new jobs. However, the physical property is owned by the city in which it is located. The grantee in this case is the county in which the project will be located. The actual shop owner will not necessarily receive any benefit because the space will be leased. It will be up to the grantee whether the lease will be made on favorable terms. However, the shop owner will be required to maintain documentation on the jobs created and prove that at least 51 percent of the jobs, as required by regulation, are given to persons of low- and moderate-income.

I have worked on other projects in which funds were provided as a grant to the jurisdiction in which the project was located and then passed through as a grant to the business. However, in these cases, the amount of private investment was at least eight or nine times the amount of the federal assistance, which was used as "gap financing."

The final type of assistance is in-kind, or direct services provided without any actual funds going from the funding agency to the grantee. Much of the assistance in this category is provided as what is called "technical assistance," or professional help to study a particular problem.

More commonly, applicants may provide in-kind contributions as the local match for a particular project. For example, staff may work on the administration of a grant, and the value of their time is then counted as a contribution to the project. In addition, professionals may contribute their expertise either totally free of charge or at a reduced cost. On certain occasions, donations of materials may be accepted.

Many communities that are novices to the grant writing field do not think to factor in the cost of their time and materials to administer a grant. However, their resources will be needed in order to see the grant through to completion. I have seen cases where the time of the policymakers on city and county councils is added into the budget. Their role in providing general oversight and supervision carries a cost. They will be called upon to review and sign the grant application, possibly hold a public hearing, settle any problems that arise during the course of the project, approve the award of any contracts associated with the grant, approve disbursements, and sign off on any final reports. Obviously, any review by an elected body also involves staff time in preparing background material and briefing the officials.

GOVERNMENT AND PRIVATE FUNDING

Most government funding comes from either the federal or state governments. In general, most municipalities and county governments do not provide grant funds. However, it may be that the county governments are given an allocation from the state for a particular purpose, and they, in turn, hand it down to municipalities or nonprofits.

I am not aware of any local governments making grants through a regular solicitation of applications. Many city and county governments do provide funding from their budgets to various nonprofits and local groups. This is not considered grant making, per se, but rather part of the budgetary process.

Private funding is supplied by wealthy individuals, corporations, banks, and foundations. A "foundation" is a nonprofit organization with a board of directors and trustees that provides funds for various charitable causes. Most foundations have been organized under federal or state charters. Others have been organized under trust agreements. It is very difficult to give the reader generalities about government funding versus private funding. Just as soon as I think of broad brush statements, I can think of an exception. However, the following generalities in regard to private foundation funding apply pretty much across the board:

- Most foundations will accept a brief letter of inquiry as the initial contact, whereas with government sources, letters of inquiry are never used. The applicant will submit either a pre-application or an application. The pre-application can sometimes be as lengthy as an application.
- Many foundations accept inquiries throughout the year. This is also true of some governmental sources. However, governmental sources are more likely to have a specific period of time when they will accept applications. In many cases, this is done once a year.
- Private foundations are less likely to have specific, concrete rating and ranking systems with points assigned to various factors. Most government sources of funds spell out very precisely how they will rate and rank an application.
- Private foundations are more prone to making decisions based on personal factors. These could include having personal knowledge of the applying organization or being personally acquainted with one of its staff members.
- Most foundations tend to have less complex requirements for grant administration. In some cases, a final report may be required. Nearly all federal and state funding agencies require some sort of formalized reporting procedure and may have other administrative requirements that must be followed.

- In line with the idea that foundations are freer to choose their grant-ees without benefit of a formal rating system, some only give grants to preselected organizations. The family or individuals funding the foundation may have an interest in certain subject matter and wish to support only that particular cause.
- Most foundations are not able to make large grants and, in general, support smaller projects.
- Foundations are not under the same scrutiny as state and local government funding programs and, thus, are freer to utilize their own rules and regulations. Federal and state funding sources must abide by the laws governing their grant programs as well as the regulations that have been developed to ensure that those laws are followed. This gives private foundations a much greater degree of internal control. Governmental agencies are bound by the strictures put into place by Congress and the various state legislatures.

Overall, I have found it much easier to search for federal and state programs rather than foundation funding. One reason for this is that there is a limited universe of governmental funding sources. There are only so many federal government agencies and state agencies. This makes it much easier to search this specific set of possibilities. In addition, with the requirement that information about governmental sources be completely public, this data is much more readily available. A relatively experienced researcher may find government funding programs fairly quickly using search tools that are free of charge.

Sources such as the Catalog of Federal Domestic Assistance and the Web site http://www.grants.gov make it much easier for the researcher. If one is familiar with the various key words in the grant writing field, it is possible to do a methodical search within a reasonable period of time.

However, searching for private foundations that may be possibilities for funding is considerably more complicated and may take much more time and expense. It is very difficult, if not impossible, to do a free search of foundations on the Internet. Searching on various key words for your type of project will not yield a list of foundations. Instead, what will come up will be a number of articles about individual foundations that have funded projects similar to what the searcher is looking for. Most tools that search for foundations require the payment of a fee, whether the listing is online or in hard copy.

PROFESSIONAL ASSOCIATIONS

I would strongly recommend that the aspiring or experienced grant writer join a professional association. This provides a great opportunity for networking, obtaining reliable information on grant seeking and grant writing, and the chance to hear about current and future training opportunities. Membership in a professional association affords the grant writer the chance to stay abreast of the latest news in the grant world and also provides the professional support, which is so important. Working in a vacuum is never recommended. In my opinion, the membership dues are money well spent.

The following are national professional associations for grant writers:

- American Grant Writers' Association (http://www.agwa.us)
- American Association of Grant Professionals (http://grantprofes sionals.org)

Many of the larger metropolitan areas are home to regional or local professional associations. A Google search will yield the name and contact information for the association closest to home.

In addition to professional associations for grant writers, there are also professional associations for grant makers. The Forum of Regional Associations of Grant Makers (http://www.givingforum.org) is a national organization that gives professional support to regional associations of grant makers. The group has 33 members representing 4,000 foundations, corporations, organizations, and individuals. This umbrella group provides support through classes, publications, opportunities for networking, and dissemination of information regarding employment opportunities. The forum basically serves as a collective voice for grant makers. The Web site states very specifically that no services are provided to grant seekers.

The regional associations of grant seekers serve the same functions for their local members—organizing networking events, providing education opportunities, acting as an information resource, and serving as a conduit to communicate the value of philanthropy to local, state, and national leaders as well as the media. The reader is directed to the Web site of the Washington (D.C.) Regional Association of Grant Makers (http://www.washingtongrant makers.org) to see a good example of the functions performed by regional associations of grant makers. This group has developed a common application form that its members may use in their giving process. It operates two programs of its own—one to fund economic development projects and the other to fund projects fighting HIV/AIDS. These programs are set up as funding collaboratives.

WHAT YOU ARE GETTING INTO—OBLIGATIONS THAT COME WITH GRANTS

I realize that I am stating the obvious, but it is absolutely necessary to read carefully through the program solicitation for funds and the complete application in order to see what your organization's obligations will be both at the time of application submittal and during the life of the grant. Most solicitations make this abundantly clear during the application process. The majority of federal and state agencies, as well as private foundations, spell this out completely in the application package.

There is another reason to read this material carefully, other than knowing what the applicant will get into, and that is checking for any problem areas that would disqualify the application. Your organization may not be able to afford the local match, you may not be an eligible applicant, or your project may not be an eligible activity.

Most governmental grants have what is called "certifications" and/or "assurances," which spell out specifically the federal laws that must be followed as well as any reporting requirements. This is sometimes also the case with private foundations, although they are more likely to have this material contained in the grant agreement that comes after the grant is awarded.

The grant agreement is a complete listing of the obligations of the grantee. In many cases, there is a requirement that any publicity in regard to the project must mention that the funding was provided by the specific agency giving the grant. In addition, grant agreements generally spell out the following:

- term of the grant
- amount awarded
- requirements for drawing funds
- reporting requirements
- recordkeeping requirements, including the length of time the records must be maintained
- obligations of the grantee in regard to program beneficiaries, or those who will benefit from the project
- requirements for sustaining the project once the grant period has expired
- requirements for program evaluation, if applicable
- contact information for the agency providing the funding
- information regarding any mandatory or voluntary grant training
- any additional requirements that must be met prior to drawing funds

There appears to be a great deal of confusion regarding the obligations of grantees. The perception exists that grant administration is extremely difficult and is often not worth the funds received. I would dispute this with great vigor. It is merely a matter of the simple principle of understanding what must be done and in what order. Most agencies are happy to walk the administrator through every step of the process. It is much easier for them to give the technical assistance while the grant is being carried out than to have to sort out the mess later on.

Please be assured that there is nothing overly onerous or complicated about administering a grant. More importantly, do not let this discourage you from seeking grants. You will be doing your organization a great disservice if you fall prey to the fear of administering government funds. I once encountered a public works director who was eager to apply for funds for street work through several programs offered by the state transportation funding agency. She asked me about the obligations that come with grants. The town manager had expressed some reservations about receiving grants because he was of the opinion that "grants are sometimes more trouble than benefit." I assured her that for the particular program we were discussing, the only obligation was for quarterly reports. For one grant, I estimated that the total time involved in preparing these reports was no more than two hours for the entire package of reports. Evidently, the town considered this to be too much trouble. However, they could have received funding for needed street repairs.

I am using this illustration in order to encourage the grant seeker to not be intimidated by the world of grant administration and to not assume that the requirements and obligations are impossible to meet. I would encourage anyone to move forward, taking these obligations seriously, but not missing out on all of the grant money that is to be had.

The following chapters will enable the grant seeker to find monies for their projects and to administer them effectively. What a reward it is to see the happy smiles of the people who have benefited from the project! This is what we do it for.

Chapter Two

Being Clear about Your Need: What Needs Fixing?

DEVELOPING CRITICAL AND "BIG PICTURE" THINKING

Developing critical and "big picture" thinking is one of the most important and useful life skills one could possibly have. Such an orientation would help anyone regardless of what profession he was in. This mindset requires thinking outside the box and the ability to get right to the heart of a problem and come up with ways to fix it. Obviously, having this trait helps the grant writer in several major ways: this type of thinking will prove invaluable in determining just what the problem is, the underlying factors causing the problem, and ways to solve the problem. This is the rock-solid foundation upon which successful grant applications are made. There is nothing mysterious about it. When you really think about it, one can see intuitively that this makes sense and that projects should be developed in a rational sequence with a clear beginning, middle, and end.

I am pleased to have the acquaintance of a very talented English instructor who has also written some poetry. He is also the organizer of a local literary discussion group. He commented to me that critical thinking is not really taught or even welcomed at the university level. In his opinion, many students today are lacking adequate skills in reading, researching, and writing, all of which require the individual to throw aside common wisdom when warranted. In his observation, many educational systems in the United States merely want to teach a block of facts by rote. Much of the material is assimilated through memory. However, these memories fade in time and do not form the foundation of a real education.

Before I begin to relate this to grant writers, I would like to give a few examples of how students can think outside the box and create new paradigms. The reader will then be able to better understand how this skill can be used in grant writing. One example would be history. The problem is that history is written by people. There is, thus, the potential for an inadvertent or intentional slant toward a certain viewpoint or mistakes in interpreting the original resource materials. The student of history must always keep this in mind and question those facts that do not make sense. A good example of people using critical thinking is those scientists who developed quantum physics. This branch of science came into being when it was noticed that conventional physics could not explain certain things at the atomic level. Quantum physics is now generally accepted as a credible body of work that is constantly evolving. If those scientists had not used critical thinking, they would have merely dismissed those aspects of nature that could not be explained by conventional physics.

In the grant field, critical thinking is absolutely necessary. The caveat here is to take nothing for granted. I would like to point out several areas where grant writers should think critically. These are just examples, and it is incumbent upon the grant writer to use this type of big picture thinking in all aspects of their work. These examples are as follows:

- Do not assume that what has worked in another place will work in yours. It is necessary to consider how the geographic location of that project affected the results. If that is the case, then it might not be completely transferable to your area.
- Do not assume that intangibles do not count in a project. Not everything can be measured in a scientific and mathematical way. Most projects do not take into account how individual will (or lack thereof) can affect the results. This is particularly true in projects having a social services component. An after-school program may not take into account students who are unusually ambitious and dedicated.
- Do not assume that the staff of your agency necessarily has the capacity to carry out a particular project. It is necessary for the grant writer to mentally put herself and her colleagues into the picture of the new project and try to visualize the various pitfalls as well as strengths there might be in a given situation.
- Do not assume that commonly accepted remedies to problems are always the best way to go. One of the best examples of this is working to create new jobs in a community and not being selective about what types of companies come in. Always putting the creation of new jobs ahead of environmental considerations will, in the long run, be detrimental to the community.

THE IMPORTANCE OF LOOKING AT THE PROBLEM FIRST

Sometimes, believe it or not, it is difficult to actually identify what the real problem is. Grant writers deal with the full range of social, economic, and environmental problems. Governmental entities may deal with a lack of public infrastructure, a high crime rate, poor economic indicators, lack of recreational facilities, public health concerns, weaknesses in the public education system, and the need to preserve cultural and historic resources. Nonprofits typically deal with the need for supplemental educational activities, the need for assistance to destitute individuals, sports and after-school programs, the need for job and life skills training and mentoring, housing problems, the natural environment, and a whole host of other needs that are not met by governmental entities.

In many situations, the problem is clear. A good example would be a city government that might be aware of a street that is in need of sidewalk repair or replacement. Obviously the need exists to either build a new sidewalk or repair the old one. Likewise, the consequences of the problem are also obvious. In this example, the deteriorated condition of the sidewalk leads to unsafe conditions, which include the risk that elderly or frail individuals may trip or fall. The unsightly condition of the sidewalks may contribute to neighborhood blight, which in turn lowers property values and causes economic problems for the residents.

An outdated sewage treatment plant will lead to a lack of capacity for new development, which hinders the economic growth of an area. In addition, the poor condition of the plant may result in inefficient service to the residents and cause higher user fees. The repair of the plant or the construction of a new one will solve the problem. In both examples given, the problem is easy to identify. Existing infrastructure is not adequate to serve the needs of the residents. Once this infrastructure is repaired or replaced, the problem is resolved.

Other types of projects require a more thoughtful approach to identifying the problem. Let us take the case of a nonprofit that wishes to find a way to lower the high dropout rate at the high schools in its area. The high dropout rate is what I call "the presenting problem" or the end result of other societal problems. These other problems include what society as a whole assumes to be the cause of the presenting problem—lack of familial encouragement; devaluation at home of the merits of education; lack of economic resources, thus resulting in a need for the student to work in addition to going to school; lack of other wholesome activities for youth in the community; and living in a high crime atmosphere, which makes it difficult to study.

These are actually the underlying causes of the high dropout rate, according to common wisdom as well as documented studies. The nonprofit that is looking for a way to resolve the problem will need to tailor the program to address the underlying causes. For example, the program may include coursework on the value of getting a good education in order to counteract the opposite attitude prevalent at home. It is much more difficult to address the crime and economic issues. This is where the nonprofit may wish to co-operate with the local law enforcement agency in order to bring about more police presence in the neighborhood in which the youth live. A well-designed program may also link the parents, job services, and job training in order to eliminate the economic stress being felt by the student and his or her family.

This example was given in order to demonstrate how one specific issue, that is, the dropout rate, cannot be addressed without working specifically on the underlying causes. In some cases, additional tutoring alone can be enough to reduce the number of dropouts. However, the most effective programs offer multiple services to address multiple causes. This is why it is important to dig a little further in order to identify the underlying causes of the problem. Research into the design of similar programs across the country can and must be undertaken. However, it is essential to take into account factors that are unique to your area. This process may sound somewhat complex, but it greatly adds to the chances for success of a project.

THE PERILS OF "PUTTING THE CART BEFORE THE HORSE"

In this context, "putting the cart before the horse" refers to a process whereby applicants decide they want something regardless of whether it is really needed. These people do not do a need assessment or look critically at the problem in order to design a project that will be effective. It is not wise to apply for more funding than is actually needed. This is most often the case with requests for equipment.

A professional friend in one of the western states related to me a situation that particularly bears upon this. One public safety agency, hearing that another community had successfully used a video surveillance system to cut crime, decided that they wanted to do the same thing. The other community found that this equipment took the place of additional manpower and was therefore effective in deterring crime. That community, with a population of a little over 5,000, had 7 cameras placed around town. The second police agency, serving a town of approximately 4,800, decided they wanted to apply for a system costing $150,000 with 15 cameras. This was clearly overkill. My friend's knowledge of the town convinced him that there were not 15 high crime areas there. It was a mystery what they would do with all of those cameras. However, some agencies want the best and latest technology whether they need it or not. Unfortunately, some agencies want to win a competition with other agencies as to who has the best equipment.

Using this example, it is evident that a needs assessment was not performed. Although it had been documented that video surveillance equipment, by its very nature, deters crime due to the fact that potential perpetrators do not want to be caught on tape, the community did not engage in critical thinking to look at their town and determine how many cameras they really needed. A well-designed project would have started with a comparison of the crime statistics in different parts of the town in order to determine trends, such as the percentage of increase or decrease in crime as well as the types of crime prevalent in each neighborhood. This information could have been used to determine how many cameras were needed and where they should be placed. It would have been necessary to look at the types of crime due to the fact that surveillance cameras placed on the street are more likely to catch crimes against property, drug deals, and street assaults. Other types of crime, such as those occurring more often in the home, would not be caught on tape. Needless to say, this project did not get funded despite several attempts.

Another example of "putting the cart before the horse," or identifying "wants" rather than needs, are agencies who want to apply for equipment to place in every single agency vehicle. For example, in any law enforcement department's fleet there are those vehicles that are too old to be used regularly, those used by the Chief and other top-ranking officers who do not patrol or make traffic stops, and those that are surplus. Obviously a department will have only a certain percentage of their vehicles on the road at any given time. I have been told about several instances of departments who wanted to apply for funds to place cutting-edge equipment in every vehicle. Naturally, they were not able to procure grant funds to do this. Most funding agencies are savvy enough to know that putting equipment into one-third to one-half of a department's vehicles will allow nearly all officers on any given shift to use it.

My final example refers to departments who apply for equipment when they really do not need it at all. I read an account of a rural fire department in the Midwest that applied for funding to replace two-year-old hoses that had barely been used. Their reasoning was that they should apply for *something* because a specific grant program was open for applications. This is a big waste of resources and could divert funding away from other departments that really need the money. As in the other two examples, no grant funds were awarded.

By this time, the reader should have gotten the idea that applications not documenting a specific and credible need do not get funded. This is pretty universal in the grant world. Grant writers and administrators should make sure that they really need the resources they are requesting.

LOOKING AT FAMILIAR THINGS WITH A FRESH EYE

Human nature is such that we continue to think in the same ways we have always thought. Certain patterns get embedded in our consciousness, and it is difficult to extract them. Looking at things with a fresh eye means that we are willing to examine a problem without prejudice and are willing to turn our world upside down if need be. This type of thinking is an attitude, rather than a skill.

It is quite difficult to change long-cherished attitudes. This involves the complete dismantling of the way one thinks about his or her work. I will give an example in order to clarify. Suppose a social service agency has been operating a program to teach low- and moderate-income persons job interview skills, with mixed results. This program involves passing out educational materials, giving classes, and doing some one-on-one mentoring. The agency continues to operate their program in this manner because all other such agencies around the country are doing the same thing. However, it is obvious that the program is not working as well as intended. The percentage of clients getting and keeping good jobs is only 30 percent, when the agency had hoped for a 60 percent success rate.

It is necessary for the agency to redesign the program so as to achieve better results. This can only be done by starting at the beginning and working to plumb the minds of the clients in order to determine why the educational effort is not working. It could be that lack of self-esteem is undermining the positive effects of the job interview skills education. The current design of the project is only going to be able to accomplish so much unless the lack of self confidence is addressed. One possible solution for this is to beef up the self-esteem module of the program. It could be that not enough time was devoted to this very important aspect of job seeking.

If something needs to be fixed, the best way to do so is to figuratively take it apart piece by piece to see where the problem lies. The most efficient way to do this is to examine the project from the foundation on up. When agency staff changes their attitudes to look at things with a fresh eye, the answer generally becomes clear.

Chapter Three

Designing a Project: How to Make It More Fundable

COMMON RULES THAT APPLY TO MOST GRANTS

Once the grant writer has clearly identified the need, the next step is to decide what activities can be undertaken in order to meet that need. This sounds like a very commonsense step, and indeed it is. First and foremost, the activity or activities must "work." Sometimes this is a matter of common sense and sometimes it is speculative. One of the major tasks in writing any grant application is to demonstrate that the problem will be solved utilizing the methodology proposed.

Once a grant writer feels confident that this can be demonstrated, there are several other elements that should be considered in designing the project. These elements are as follows: cost-effectiveness, sustainability, ease with which the project can be evaluated, documented success of similar projects or promise as a pilot, and eligibility for a wide range of funding programs. Taking the measure of these other factors is especially important if there are several different possibilities that could work.

An example will serve to clearly illustrate the overall picture in choosing a project to fill the need and meet the elements described previously. Let us say that a community action agency in a major city is aware that the teenage pregnancy rate is rising at an alarming rate. What can they do about it? This can only be determined by deciding what is causing the situation. The local social services department keeps data on the teenage mothers that it serves. This data is collected to be put into a report that evaluates the information given by the mothers.

Perhaps it becomes obvious that lack of education and teenage pregnancy are highly correlated. The community action agency then decides to print literature and to hold classes in conjunction with the social services department in order to combat the lack of education, which may be a factor in causing the high pregnancy rate. They decide to print brochures that are relatively inexpensive and partially utilize their own staff to teach the classes in order to cut down costs. The agency then approaches the county government to fund this program for a certain number of years once grant funds from other funding agencies are exhausted. They then devise a measurement tool to compare teenage pregnancy rates before and after the first year of operation of this program. They can then claim cost efficiency, research that proves the need, sustainability, and ease of evaluation. This project will thus be a funder's dream.

DEVELOPING ACTIVITIES THAT DIRECTLY AND CLEARLY MEET THE IDENTIFIED NEED

In many cases finding activities that fill the need is easy. If there are potholes in a street, the obvious solution is to fill them in. If a road's rough surface causes a rise in the number of accidents, then the road must be resurfaced. If the playground equipment at a city park is very old and in danger of breaking with children on it, it is clear that new equipment must be purchased.

Other needs often have at least two solutions and sometimes more. In the example in the previous section, the data supported the possibility that lack of education was contributing to the teenage pregnancy rate. However, the lack of access to birth control could have easily been determined to be the major factor. In that case distributing contraceptives would have been the answer.

Following, I give two examples of a problem with more than one possible root cause and activities that can be designed to address those root causes. The first problem is an increasing rate of homelessness. Possible causes and their solutions are as follows:

- A generally poor economy is providing a less than optimum number of jobs. In this case, an economic development program aimed at attracting new business would create new jobs and therefore reduce homelessness.
- Homelessness is tied to substance abuse. A program to reach homeless people and attempt to provide counseling and treatment for their addictions will help to alleviate the problem.
- Homelessness is also tied to mental illness. In this case, a counseling and treatment program aimed at the homeless will help.

The community action agency that wishes to help will need to study the homeless population very carefully and determine which of the above would be more helpful. In many cases, more than one root cause is attacked. The agency may very well determine that bringing in a significant number of new jobs is beyond its capability. Or it is possible that the agency may partner with the city's economic development department in order to beef up efforts to attract additional business. There is also the immediate need of providing shelter for the homeless people. Although not a root cause of homelessness, the lack of shelter makes it difficult to serve that population. The agency may very well decide to apply for funds to develop a new homeless shelter that will provide treatment for addictions and mental illness.

My second example involves an alarming increase in burglaries in a particular city. The following have been identified as possible root causes.

- The perpetrators have become aware that the police department has limited resources and thus feel freer to commit crimes.
- The citizens of the area, becoming more afraid due to the spike in burglaries, are afraid to approach the police for fear of retaliation.
- The police department has been stretched thin in responding to crimes of violence in other parts of the city.
- Due to hard economic times, the city has had to lay off several officers, thus reducing the amount of time that can be spent on patrol.

In this case, it is pretty clear that lack of police resources is a major issue. The question then is whether the police department should apply for (1) funding to create new officer positions, (2) funding for overtime, or (3) funding to purchase equipment that would take the place of additional manpower. It is evident that a detailed analysis and assessment of the particular situation in that city should be completed by the police agency or by a consulting professional in order to determine what approach will be the most effective. In any case, even if the equipment is chosen, this is still being done with an eye toward increasing the manpower on the street.

It all comes down to logical thinking. It is important to think critically in order to identify all of the possible causes of a particular problem. The final challenge in designing the project is to determine which solution will be the most effective. The best means of making this difficult decision is obtaining the most comprehensive research data available and analyzing it for its applicability to your specific problem.

PROJECT DESIGN AND THE NEED
TO DEMONSTRATE SUSTAINABILITY

Some grant applicants have no idea how they will continue the project once grant funds have been exhausted. If they had adequate funds in the first place, there would be no need to seek grants. Many funding agencies understand this dilemma and do not turn down a good project just because it can only be funded for a one-year period. Their thinking is that it is better to make a moderate impact on a problem for a specific timeframe than it is to do nothing at all.

However, it is a big mistake to not address this issue in the grant application. I would recommend that the grant writer always at least state that other grants will be sought in order to continue the program. This will sound even more credible if a few examples of other potential funding sources are given. In lieu of this, the grant search tools the applicant will use should be specified in the application.

It is okay to state that the applicant will assess its own budget to see if funds will be available to continue the project. It may very well be that financial conditions will improve. Or it may be that the applicant just decides that so much progress has been made that the money must be found somewhere to continue the project.

Of course, it is always desirable to be able to point out that there is a definite identified source of funds beyond the grant period. For example, a local nonprofit may receive a commitment from the county government to fund a program for two years beyond the life of the grant.

Sustainability is not nearly as important in the case of the purchase of equipment or the rehabilitation of a building. In these cases, the equipment or the building has a useful life of many years. Some grant programs will request information regarding how the applicant will meet operating expenses associated with this type of program.

DESIGNING A PROJECT THAT CAN BE EASILY EVALUATED

Nearly every funding agency wants to know that the project will be successful. If that were not the case, there would be no point in their providing grant funds. Most grant applications therefore require that the applicant spell out how they will measure the success of their project. Simply put, it must be demonstrated that the problem is either alleviated completely or some sort of positive impact is made. Generally, this is demonstrated with statistical information. There is nothing wrong, however, with also including anecdotal information. This can often give the "human" element behind the numbers.

One of the best examples of this is the increase in the feelings of security and safety among residents of a high crime neighborhood once a crime prevention program has been implemented. This is something that is very difficult to measure using statistics.

The evaluation process should be considered when choosing among several alternative activities rather than choosing an activity and then fitting a measurement tool around that activity. The grant writer should carefully review the data that is available to be used for evaluation. In the case of a program involving services to individuals, the impact upon those persons' lives should be measured and form the basis of an evaluation. For example, a job training program can easily track the number of trainees who receive jobs appropriate to their level of training.

Nearly all evaluation efforts involve collecting data throughout the course of the project. Often it is tempting to spend time on implementing the project rather than taking the time to see what is happening. However, it is absolutely necessary to take this approach for two reasons. First, your results will be helpful to other organizations in their project design. Second, if you find that your project works well, you will want to continue with it as originally designed and search for additional funds to increase the good that has been done.

You may wish to consider engaging the services of an outside agency to evaluate your project. There are consulting firms that provide this service. Stating in the application that an outside evaluator will be used will improve your chances for funding. In some cases, this expense can be charged to the grant. The funding agency will see that you are totally committed to the project because you are willing to commit to hire an evaluator to do an impartial and accurate review. It is possible that your local university or community college may be able to assist in evaluating your project for no charge or at a reduced fee. It is also wise to contact nonprofits and quasi-public agencies that may be able to evaluate the project for a smaller fee than a consultant.

The questions to be answered during an evaluation are very obvious and basic, as follows:

- Did the project achieve its purposes?
- Was it completed on time?
- Were a sufficient amount of resources devoted to the project?
- Were all activities completed successfully?
- If there were beneficiaries, was there a sense that they realized a benefit?

Well-designed evaluations generally involve some sort of stakeholder input. At the end of the project, the grantee could consider designing a questionnaire that would be answered by the project beneficiaries and other interested parties. It is best to interject some quantitative data into this questionnaire in order to standardize it.

BENEFICIARY AND PUBLIC INPUT

A few grant programs, such as CDBG and some programs of the U.S. Department of Justice, require that public input be obtained prior to submitting the application. This requirement applies mainly to programs where the applicants are local governments and states. For the most part, this requirement is satisfied by holding a public hearing with adequate notice to the public. This sort of input is sought from all citizens of the jurisdiction.

Other programs require that potential beneficiaries have an opportunity to comment upon program design. This may be as simple as inviting all of the clients of a local social services agency to comment if they wish. Another way to approach this may be to *require* that any beneficiaries receiving assistance answer this questionnaire. This may be done before program design is completed in order that beneficiaries may have the maximum influence on the development of the project. In other cases, the applicant agency may merely ask its beneficiaries to comment upon the proposed project once it has been developed. Naturally, input from any beneficiaries is more useful prior to finalizing the project design. Their viewpoints as to the extent of the need and what would help the most can make the critical difference between a successful project and one that fails to accomplish its objectives.

COLLABORATION WITH OTHER AGENCIES

Funding agencies are increasingly giving additional points in the rating to projects that will be operated by two or more agencies. The rationale here is that such projects are more likely to be successful due to having combined expertise and resources. The advantages of collaborating with another agency to improve the project are as follows:

- The amount of the local cash and/or in-kind match can be increased.
- Each agency can bring its own special area of expertise to bear.
- Having additional staff available to implement the project is a benefit.
- A greater number of beneficiaries may be reached.
- Additional resources for sustainability and evaluation are available.

On the downside, collaborative projects mean that individual agencies do not have complete control of a project. This is a real problem when one or more of the agencies do an inadequate job of administering their portion of the project. It can be very hard to shake the poor impression that your association with such a partner can make. Needless to say, it is essential to choose your partners with care. It is preferable to align yourself only with those agencies with whose work you are entirely familiar.

Regardless of the number of agencies that may collaborate on a project, in many cases, the grant maker prefers that only one be the actual applicant. That agency would be the one to sign the grant agreement and undertake the financial administration. Of course, the applicant is responsible for any problems and must ensure that the other agencies fulfill their roles properly.

A collaborative project is somewhat different from one in which there is a subrecipient relationship. In this case, the applicant would be responsible for dispersing funds and monitoring adherence to administrative requirements. However, the subrecipient would do most of the work in actually implementing the project. An example of this would be a county government that receives funds to undertake a housing rehabilitation program. A local community action agency may be the group that actually takes applications from lower income families, chooses the beneficiaries, and sees that the rehabilitation work is done properly. That agency would be referred to as a subrecipient. The county would disperse the funds to the community action agency. It is generally up to the grant recipient how much control they have over the project beyond that.

A QUICK CHECKLIST TO DETERMINE THE CHANCES OF GETTING FUNDING FOR A PROJECT

This checklist is being provided so that the grant writer may see how the proposed activity meets the characteristics of a well-designed project. Granted, I have seen several cases where an activity that does not meet all the criteria has received funding. The project may be very strong in several key areas but weak in one or two others and still get funded. Many times funders are moved by what seems to them to be the greater good to be served and go on to approve a project that is not "perfect."

After considering the rest of the information in this chapter and designing a project that you think is a fundable one, take a few minutes to see how the project stacks up with the items on the checklist. Rather than just checking off each applicable criterion, assign each one a value of from one to five, with one being the minimum measurement of that criteria and five being the most. For example, a project may lend itself to only limited measurement and evaluation. The grant writer may then decide to assign this factor a "two," while a project that can be easily measured and analyzed statistically may be assigned a "five." This is just another way to test your proposed activity to see the likelihood of its getting funded. The grant writer will get more accurate results by assigning a degree of measurement to each criterion rather than merely knowing whether it exists.

This checklist is as follows:

- ❐ The problem will be fully or partially solved.
- ❐ The project is ready to proceed.
- ❐ The project will be completed in a timely fashion.

❏ Matching funds have been committed.

❏ The applicant has a commitment for funding to sustain the project once the grant period is completed or sustainability will occur through project design such as for a new construction project or an equipment purchase.

❏ The applicant can demonstrate that an exhaustive search of other sources was conducted.

❏ The proposed activity has worked elsewhere for a similar problem.

❏ The activity was developed after looking at several alternatives.

❏ The results of the project are easily measured.

❏ An evaluation plan is in place and the appropriate resources have been secured.

❏ The project has support from the general public, the population to be served, professionals who work in the field, and governmental entities in whose jurisdiction it will take place.

❏ The applicant has a proven track record in administering similar projects and there have been no problems in the administration of previous grants.

❏ Collaborative agreements have been secured.

❏ Construction and rehabilitation activities have been at least partially designed.

❏ Any professional studies specific to this project have been completed.

❏ Cost estimates have been carefully documented.

❏ The project is included in the appropriate planning documents.

❏ Statistical data has been used to document the need and is included with the application.

❏ A feasible work plan can be developed for inclusion in the application.

❏ Any procurement activities can be conducted so as to meet the requirements of the granting agency.

❏ It can be demonstrated that the activity chosen is clearly superior to other alternatives.

Chapter Four

Searching for Grant Sources

SEARCH TECHNIQUES

I have found that search resources and techniques are constantly changing and evolving. It is necessary for the grant seeker to continually stay abreast of new search tools in order to be able to locate all potential sources of funding. There are a considerable number of free search resources. Some of these are print materials that can be found in local and college libraries. However, online search tools have become the norm. Often, community foundations will share their search tools with local nonprofits. For example, the Community Foundation of the Eastern Shore, located in Salisbury, Maryland, has a subscription to the Foundation Center Online. Nonprofits are welcome to come to the office and review this database, along with the extensive library.

Nonprofit organizations looking for foundation money will either need to invest in fee-based search tools or have a wonderful support system in the form of larger organizations that will allow them to borrow their search tools. Many of the search tools for federal and state grants are free. Local governments are in an enviable position. Because most of their funding comes from specific federal and state governments, it is much easier to identify the agencies that can help with their projects. Most of my clients are municipalities and counties, and I very seldom have to do an extensive grant search for them. For example, there are only certain agencies and programs that fund water and sewer projects located in my state. These include the Community Development Block Grant Program, the Maryland Department of the Environment, the U.S. Environmental Protection Agency, and the U.S. Department of Agriculture. Law enforcement agencies here receive the majority of their funding from the U.S. Department of Justice and the Maryland Governor's Office of Crime Control and Prevention. Smaller law enforcement projects may also receive funding from local foundations, banks, businesses, and service clubs.

Fortunately, the grant seeker will find a plethora of search resources. This is due in part to the pervasive availability of electronic information. We are in the enviable position of having to spend a significant amount of time weeding out grant search tools and potential funding agencies, rather than having to work hard to ferret out this information. It is a matter of learning to work efficiently and utilizing those search tools that will give the most "bang for the buck." This could also be expressed as "learning to work smarter, not harder." Of course, the beginning grant writer will need to take time to learn which search tools provide the most reliable and easy-to-access information. Learning the art of discrimination in this area does take time. Do not be discouraged if you feel at first as if your energy is being scattered in a dozen directions. With patience and diligent work, the grant writer will learn how to make the most effective use of time when doing a grant search.

Persons searching for grants should be thorough and search all of the applicable tools discussed in this chapter. It is particularly tempting to quit searching after a couple of what appear to be very good sources have been found. Unless all of the search resources are looked at, it is likely that the researcher will miss other possibilities that may be even better.

When doing a search, it is often possible to specify "and," "or," and "not" to modify your search criteria to better locate what you are looking for. Exactly how you do this depends on the system you are using. Most search engines have an "advanced" search function that lets the researcher specifically put in a series of words that either all have to be present, or only one of which has to be present. If you want to use a simple search and want everything to be included, put the specific words to be searched in quotation marks. Most search engines will understand that the entire phrase needs to be there. If the searcher inputs a series of words or phrases separated by commas, the search engine will look for them individually, giving first the results that combine the most of the words/phrases first with the following results having less and less of them together.

The researcher should be careful to not use common words that would get picked up by most potential results. Try to not use "the," "and" (unless it's a system where "and" actually specifies wanting two or more things at the same time), "for," or any other small common word. If it is in quotation marks this is not as big a problem as it will often search for the entire phrase lined up just as the searcher entered it, but adding unnecessary words is generally a bad idea and learning not to add them will go far in helping you find what you want.

Grant searches are not always merely a technical exercise. Some of my most successful searches have yielded results when I have played a hunch and called a colleague for ideas. It sometimes happens that a good source does not show up in the grant search. Contacting someone who you know has had a similar project funded may yield the name of an obscure foundation that is a perfect fit for your project. Common sense is very effective here. I very rarely do a grant search where I do not sit down and consciously try to "think outside of the box," and call those people who come to mind. Please read on and enjoy being pleasantly surprised at the vast number of grant search resources at your disposal.

FEDERAL GRANTS

Fortunately, the grant seeker has a number of free sources to choose from in searching for federal government grants. In my opinion, Grants.gov and the Catalog of Federal Domestic Assistance (CFDA) are two of the more useful search tools, although there are others that I utilize from time to time. I will discuss the application preparation and submission component of Grants. gov in Chapter 7. However, in this chapter, I will take the reader through the methodology for utilizing this site for grant searches. One of the most effective methods for determining whether a particular federal program is a good fit is by taking note of the total amount of funding available and the number of awards that will be made. This will allow the grant seeker to determine how intense the competition will be. For example, a local nonprofit that only works within its own county does not stand a great deal of chance in a federal program that will only make three grant awards in the entire country. However, if another federal program offers a total of $50 million and expects to make 500 awards of an average $100,000 each, the nonprofit stands a much better chance of getting funded, particularly if it is proposing a well-planned project.

Grants.Gov

Grants.gov is a Web site that allows grant seekers to search for federal grant opportunities and submit applications online. It can be found at http://www. grants.gov. The Web site is managed by the U.S. Department of Health and Human Services. Forty-two federal agencies are currently listing all of their discretionary grant programs on this site. In all, the site describes more than 1,000 programs offering $500 billion in assistance. Grants.gov was founded under the 2002 E-Grants Initiative, which was part of the president's Management Agenda for that year.

I will name those agencies that have listed their grant opportunities on this site in order to give the novice grant seeker an idea of which federal agencies provide grants. It is also beneficial to search the individual Web sites of these agencies, particularly if your organization only deals with certain specific areas, such as law enforcement. If that is the case, a consistent monitoring of the Web sites of the U.S. Department of Justice and the U.S. Department of Homeland Security may be sufficient for your needs.

The agencies listed on Grants.gov are as follows:

- Agency for International Development
- Appalachian Regional Commission
- Bureau of Reclamation-South Central California area office
- Christopher Columbus Fellowship Foundation
- Corporation for National and Community Service
- Election Assistance Commission
- Environmental Protection Agency
- General Services Administration
- Institute of Museum and Library Services
- Institute of Peace
- James Madison Memorial Fellowship Foundation
- Japan—United States Friendship Commission
- Marine Mammal Commission
- Millennium Challenge Corporation
- National Aeronautics and Space Administration
- National Archives and Records Administration
- National Council on Disability
- National Credit Union Administration
- National Endowment for the Arts
- National Endowment for the Humanities
- National Science Foundation
- Nuclear Regulatory Commission
- Office of the Director of National Intelligence
- President's Committee on the Arts and Humanities
- Small Business Administration
- Social Security Administration
- U.S. Department of Agriculture
- U.S. Department of Commerce
- U.S. Department of Defense
- U.S. Department of Education
- U.S. Department of Energy
- U.S. Department of Health and Human Services
- U.S. Department of Homeland Security
- U.S. Department of Housing and Urban Development
- U.S. Department of Justice
- U.S. Department of Labor
- U.S. Department of State

- U.S. Department of Transportation
- U.S. Department of Veterans Affairs
- U.S. Department of the Interior
- U.S. Department of the Treasury
- Woodrow Wilson Center

The site clearly states that information regarding government benefits (such as Social Security), student loans, or small business startup funds is not available through Grants.gov. This site allows the grant seeker to search specifically for ARRA monies. A special section of the site shows the new grant opportunities that were posted that week. The grant seeker may browse by agency or subject matter. For night owls and workaholics, there is a 24-hour-a-day, 7-day-a-week help line. Grants.gov also offers the opportunity to receive e-mail alerts on new grant opportunities. The grant seeker may elect several options, including all new grants posted daily; new opportunities by agency or category; those based upon criteria specified by the grant seeker; or by funding opportunity number. In addition, e-mail alerts will provide grant seeking tips and discussion of current issues in the grant field. The subscriber does not need to be registered with Grants.gov to receive this information.

Beyond these capabilities, this site offers the option to do a basic search or an advanced search. The basic search requires the user to input keywords, the funding opportunity number assigned by Grants.gov, or the Catalog of Federal Domestic Assistance number. An advanced search allows the grant seeker to input data in one or more of the following fields: keyword; open, closed, or archived solicitations; funding opportunity number; Catalog of Federal Domestic Assistance number; the date the opportunity was posted; who may apply; the field of interest, meaning the topic area; the agency issuing the opportunity; category; or ARRA program.

Catalog of Federal Domestic Assistance

This resource has both print and online versions that include 64 federal agencies, including all major cabinet level departments. The home page of the CFDA (http://www.cfda.gov) allows the grant seeker to download the 2009 print edition. It is not necessary to have an account on this site in order to search the catalog or view programs. Again, there is a special section to search for ARRA programs.

A basic search can be done by inputting a keyword or program number and/or the type of assistance (grant, loan, federal contract, training, federal employment, etc.). A list of program solicitations will appear. The searcher may then click on a particular grant opportunity and receive a very complete description of that program. However, no application forms are available, and the grant seeker is referred to the specific agencies for that information.

The listing will contain all programs that make grants for certain types of projects (i.e., environmental, law enforcement, education, etc.), and whether the opportunity is currently open to accept applications. Many federal programs accept applications once a year.

Advanced searches allow the grant seeker to input the following: full text, assistance type (grant, loan, etc.), applicant eligibility, use of the assistance, beneficiary eligibility (the types of persons that the program will ultimately benefit, such as job recipients in the case of an economic development program), functional codes (agriculture, natural resources, law enforcement etc.), deadline, date modified, date published, whether the opportunity is funded by ARRA money, subject terms, and whether the opportunity is subject to the clearinghouse requirement.

Both the basic and advanced searches will produce the following information: authorization for the program, its objectives, the types of assistance available, applicant eligibility, application and award process, post-award reporting requirements, matching funds required, and timeline. A very handy user's guide can also be downloaded. In addition, clicking on specific agencies will produce a list of programs administered by that agency. The user has the ability to click on a particular program and view it separately.

It could be deduced that searching on CFDA should yield more opportunities due to the fact that there are 64 agencies available on that site and only 42 on Grants.gov. Of course, both sites contain listings for all of the major cabinet agencies. I would like to give a very interesting example of the widely varying results that can be obtained by searching both sites. I had a client who wished to open a school to train firefighters. While searching Grants.gov, I used the keyword "firefighter," "firefighting," and "firefighter training." Much to my surprise, I only got one result, a program administered by the Nuclear Regulatory Commission. On using the same terms in CFDA, I got over 600 results.

The *Federal Register*

The *Federal Register* (http://www.federalregister.gov) was one of the main federal grant search tools prior to the explosion of online resources. The Web site refers to it as "an official legal information service of the United States government." It is a division of the National Archives and Records Administration, which partners with the U.S. Government Printing Office in producing this document. The *Register* is published Monday through Friday except for federal holidays and includes information on federal regulations; laws; presidential documents; and federal organizations, programs, and activities. When I worked at the Federal Reserve Board in the mid-1970s, this document was *the* authoritative word on what was happening in the federal government. It still is one of the most important sources of news in that arena. However, the vast amounts of electronic resources that are much easier to search have pushed the *Federal Register* into the background as far as grant searches are concerned.

It is possible to do a simple search online. However, this search will only cover the publication of grant opportunities that are included in the document that day. Having the capability to search the entire universe of open grant opportunities by subject matter and other parameters, as is possible with Grants.gov and the CFDA, saves much valuable time.

The quickest and easiest way to access grant opportunities from the *Federal Register* is to sign up for the Grantsmanship Center's daily digest of grant opportunities published there. This service can be accessed at http://www.tgci.com/funding/FedToday.asp.

Grant Station

This is a very valuable resource that will give the grant seeker access to information about grants from nearly any source. This fee-based information service can be found at https://www.grantstation.com. Grant Station covers the following types of grants: federal; state; independent, family, community, and corporate foundations; corporate giving programs; faith-based grant makers; and associations with grant making programs. Information on state grants is provided in the form of links to the departments and agencies offering funding in all 50 states.

Other valuable resources on this site include information on writing proposals, additional learning resources, and an e-newsletter detailing items of interest in the grant world. A subscriber paying $89.00 per year may only have access to the publications of Grant Station. In order to search, one must pay a fee of $599.00 per year.

There are two specialized grant search tools that are used primarily by colleges and universities. The first is IRIS (Illinois Research Information Services), which can be a bit difficult to navigate until the searcher gets used to it. The subscribing institution pays a fee to join IRIS, and the staff, students, and faculty are then able to access the information on the site. This resource allows the searcher to choose from among 25 subject areas.

This resource contains over 9,000 grant opportunities in the sciences, social services, arts, and humanities. One handy feature of this resource is the IRIS Alert Service, which enables the user to complete a search profile that will enable the system to contact that user by e-mail in the future with opportunities that are compatible with the searcher's profile. More information on IRIS can be found at http://www.library.illinois.edu/iris. This system is set up so that users may not access it from their personal computers.

The second search tool is SPIN (Sponsored Programs Information Network). Once again, the subscribing institution pays a fee that allows its staff and students access on-demand. SPIN serves the research community, with subscribers being mainly medical centers, universities, institutes, and corporations. Like IRIS, this resource covers both federal and nonfederal grant opportunities, including programs available from international organizations. More information can be found at http://www.infoed.org. SPIN will provide e-mail alerts of funding opportunities available based on information provided by its users, similar to the process for IRIS. The Web site states that it is "the most widely used funding opportunity database in the world." This search tool will return information on funding programs sponsored by 6,000 government, private, and nonprofit sources. The researcher may make use of either a basic keyword or advanced Boolean search.

The Grantsmanship Center of Los Angeles, California, discussed in the next section on foundations, also shows federal sources of funding.

STATE GRANTS

All of the individual states offer a wide array of grant programs in such areas as water and sewer, transportation, parks and recreation, economic development, historic preservation, law enforcement, and fire fighting. States award grants to municipalities and counties as well as nonprofit organizations. Some states will also offer assistance to for-profit entities in support of economic development. If your organization is a nonprofit, get to know your local elected officials. It is quite possible that they will be able to supplement your list of potential funding sources by making suggestions from among the state programs with which they are familiar.

I always search for state sources of funding first. The state programs are easier to access than federal programs due to the fact that the applicant is competing only on the state level and not against other applicants around the entire country. A number of federal programs pass funds through to the individual states for distribution. Other state programs are funded solely by state revenues.

The CDBG program represents a very good example of a federal program that passes most of its funding to the states. On the federal level, these funds are administered by the U.S. Department of Housing and Urban Development. CDBG will find a wide variety of projects, including housing, economic development, social services, and infrastructure such as water and sewer and street work. To find the agency in your state that administers the program, go to the state Web site and search for the program using the terms "CDBG" or "Community Development Block Grant Program." This should yield a link to the agency that administers these funds. Alternatively, you may go to the state Web site, locate the list of state agencies, and look at those that handle housing and community development.

There are several ways to search for state grant funds without expending an inordinate amount of time. The most straightforward is to go to your state's Web site, find the state agency whose name implies that it regulates the area in which you seek to find a grant, and follow that link to the information on grants administered by that agency. If you are working for a county and wish to find grant funds for parks and recreation and notice that there is a Department of Natural Resources in your state, it could be assumed that that agency is likely to make grants in your area of interest. In general, grant writers working for local governments soon become familiar with which state agencies are possibilities for funding their projects.

There is a Web site (http://www.statelocalgov.net) that contains links to all state Web sites as well as the agencies under that state. In addition, there are also links to certain counties and municipalities. It is possible to click on the state in which you wish to search and then click again on the subject matter you are interested in. This will lead you to the appropriate agency, and it will then be possible to search for grant programs under that agency. There are also links to the executive branch departments and boards and commissions in that state, which is helpful if you already know which agency regulates the subject matter you are interested in. This site is very helpful if you are a consultant working in more than one state.

The Grantsmanship Center (http://www.tgci.com) Web site has links to each state's home page as well. Persons looking for homeland security grants that are passed to the states may go to http://www.dhs.gov/xgovt/grants to access information about each state's homeland security grant contact as well as the total amount allocated by program.

FOUNDATIONS

Several of the search resources detailed above cover foundation grants as well as government sources. I made the arbitrary decision to include those sources (Grant Station, IRIS, and SPIN) in the section on federal grant search tools.

It is much easier to locate resources that allow the grant seeker to find government grants for free than it is to find resources that allow for free private foundation searches. I am not aware of any efficient way of searching for foundation grants without paying a fee, unless your organization is lucky enough to have access to the subscription of another organization. When looking for foundation funds, it is often possible to exclude from the search those that only give to preselected organizations. These foundations do not accept applications from other than those groups they have already identified as recipients of their grant money. In other words, they pick the causes and groups to receive their money and just distribute the funds to them, rather than going through a public application process. A significant number of foundations fall into this category. If the grant seeker can eliminate them from the list at the beginning, it will save a lot of time.

Community foundations are just that, giving only in their local community, which can sometimes be several counties. Most community foundations feature the word "community" in their name, so it is possible to spot them at a glance. These foundations can be eliminated if they are located outside of the grant seeker's geographic area.

The search may yield several "family" foundations. These are often narrowly focused on the personal interests of the current or founding family members. In some cases, they only give to preselected organizations. It is sometimes difficult to tell from the name whether it is a family foundation, although the word "family" sometimes appears. The best way to tell whether this type of foundation is a match is to read the background information carefully to see whether they accept applications and whether your project is in line with its interests.

Foundation Center

The Foundation Center is the source that I most commonly use when searching for funding from private foundations due primarily to the comprehensive nature of its information. This organization has been in existence for over 50 years and offers information on 95,000 foundations and 1.7 million individual grants. However, this is merely a matter of personal preference. To check it out, go to http://www.foundationcenter.org. The following is the free information available from this organization:

- A list of the 100 wealthiest U.S. foundations, with the state that they are located in and links to each individual foundation is provided.
- A list of the amount of funding provided by subject area for each year, and the recipients receiving the largest amount of funding for each subject area is given.
- Foundation Finder—the grant seeker may locate foundations by searching either by their name, location, or their employer identification number, which is assigned by the Internal Revenue Service (IRS). Once the foundation is located, the searcher will be able to see a wealth of information, including the address, contact name, type of grant maker, IRS exemption status, assets, amount awarded in past years, and the 990 form, which is the tax form that nonprofits must file with the federal government.
- 990 Finder—the searcher may locate a particular 990 by inputting either the 990 form type, organization name, location, Employer Identification Number, and/or year. Once the 990 is located, the following information will appear on the screen: organization name, state, year, total assets, form type, number of pages, and the Employer Identification Number, as well as a link to the actual 990 form.

- Trend Tracker—the user of the service may specify up to five foundations at a time and receive information regarding how much those foundations have given over a seven-year period. This information is provided in bar graph, line graph, and table form.
- Search for Requests for Proposals—the grant seeker may search by subject or browse all of the requests for proposals listed. The Web site shows a summary of each RFP with a link to the original posted opportunity.
- Map showing grants by U.S. grant makers to groups abroad—this map is interactive and the researcher may click on specific countries to get information about the grants given in that country. This information includes the total amount given to organizations in the country, the number of grants, and the number of organizations receiving grants. A list of recipient organizations is also given, along with the number of grants received and the total amount for each. The searcher can then click on the recipient organization to see the name of the foundation that made the grant.
- Common grant application forms used by various associations of grant makers throughout the country
- Research studies showing trends in grant making

The following services are provided for a fee:

- Foundation Directory Online—the Center's signature and most inclusive product. There are five different levels of subscriptions, and the subscriber may pay on a monthly, annual, or biennial basis. The Foundation Directory Online is constantly updated and gives very comprehensive information. Search fields include the following: foundation name, foundation city, foundation state, fields of interest, geographical area served, and types of assistance awarded. Information that appears as a result of the search is as follows: contact information, including Web site; limitations on grants; geographic focus; financial data, such as total assets and amounts granted in recent years; type of grant maker; fields of interest; types of support; application information; publications; program description; Employer Identification Number; most recent IRS filings; and any other information deemed pertinent.
- Foundation Grants to Individuals Online
- Corporate Giving Online

Grant seekers may visit the regional offices of the Foundation Center in Atlanta, Cleveland, New York, San Francisco, and Washington, D.C., and receive free access to its databases, publications, books, periodicals, and videos.

In addition, personal reference assistance is provided along with classroom training. The Foundation Center also has a national network of more than 275 cooperating collections that provide the same information. The locations of these collections can be found on the Web site.

Grantsmanship Center

The Grantsmanship Center (http://www.tgci.com) is also a very useful resource. The following services are provided free of charge:

- Top Funding Sources by State—the researcher may click on a particular state on a U.S. map in order to see its top grant making foundations, community foundations, corporate giving programs, and the state government's home page.
- Occasional podcasts—various experts in the grant field discuss aspects of the grant business.
- Newsletter—this monthly online publication called, interestingly enough, *Centered*, publishes timely and informative articles on news of interest in the grant writing world.

The following services are also provided:

- Publications dealing with proposal writing
- Classes and seminars—a variety of programs are offered around the country
- *Grant Domain*—a searchable database containing federal, foundation, and corporate funding sources

Alumni of certain classes sponsored by the Grantsmanship Center have the right to access the publications and Grant Domain at no charge, as well as receive half-price tuition to a class specified by the organization and one complete proposal review. One may subscribe to Grant Domain for a fee if one is not an alumnus of one of the classes.

Fundsnet Services Online

Fundsnet Services Online (http://www.fundsnetservices.com) has offered its database of grant makers free of charge since 1996. Grant seekers are free to browse categories such as animals and wildlife, the environment, disabled interests, and arts and culture. The resulting list of foundations contains a link to their Web sites. Unfortunately, the researcher must look at each source separately to see how it fits with their project due to the fact that no other search parameters may be specified. This provides for a rather cumbersome process. Fundsnet also offers free fundraising kits and operates fundraising programs that sell such things as cookie dough, magazines, chocolate, and other items on behalf of schools and local nonprofits.

Grantsnet

Lastly, what has in the past been referred to as "Grantsnet" is now accessible at http://sciencecareers.sciencemag.org. This site offers free access to information about research funding in the sciences. Tips on job seeking and training in the sciences are also offered. The homepage contains a section titled "Featured Grants," which are presumably the grant opportunities that offer the largest amount of funding. Both foundation and federal government resources are given, with links to a summary page and the Web site of the agency offering the solicitation. An advanced search on this site will offer the grant seeker the opportunity to specify their experience level, whether they work as an individual or with an institution, the research topic, and the time frame for the due date of various program solicitations searched.

BANKS AND CORPORATIONS

In the case of banks and corporations, grant seekers should first of all look close to home. Many local banks and corporations make grants to local nonprofits for a wide variety of purposes. Most of the time, these entities do not have narrowly focused funding interests, but instead fund the gamut of projects. It would be my recommendation to contact all such firms within the grant seeker's county, unless it is extremely populous. In this case, searching for banks and corporations within the grant seeker's own city or neighborhood will usually be adequate.

If you have contacts within the bank or corporation, it is best to call them directly first and let them either handle the request personally or refer you to someone else. Banks and corporations are more likely to fund a project if they are familiar with the applicant and know their track record. I have seen cases where a simple phone call is adequate to make a funding request. However, in most cases, a letter is required.

If the grant seeker has a larger project or one that is not local in scope, a more comprehensive search is necessary. Many of the larger banks have set up independent foundations to channel their giving. All foundations, including bank foundations, are listed in the Foundation Directory Online (http://fconline.foundationcenter.org). The grant seeker will either need to purchase a subscription to this service or get permission to access someone else's subscription. Once on the site, enter the words "Corporate giving program" or "Company-sponsored foundation" in the Type of Grant Maker field. Then, in order to locate bank foundations, use the word "bank" in the Company Name field. This will yield a list of over 200 banks that have foundations.

The Foundation Center also has a very good product, Corporate Giving Online, which gives extensive information on corporate funding. This service is available for $59.95 per month and may be accessed at http:// foundationcenter.org/findfunders/fundingsources.cgo.html. This resource provides the grant seeker with information on 4,300 company-sponsored foundations and corporate giving programs. It also provides detailed profile information for over 3,600 companies. These profiles will provide contact information as well as details on how to access the funding. One important feature of this resource is information on local offices, which would generally be the point of contact. The Foundation Center reports that corporate foundations made $4.4 billion in grants in 2008.

Grant seekers should know the difference between a company-sponsored foundation and a corporate direct giving program. Company-sponsored foundations are set up as separate legal entities from the parent corporation. Even so, company policy is very influential in the giving guidelines of the foundation. The funding programs are generally supported by regular contributions from the parent company. A corporate direct giving program is an integral part of the company itself and is not incorporated separately. This type of program frequently includes employee matching gifts as part of its giving program.

The 10 largest corporate foundations in the United States are:

- Alcoa (PA)
- Fidelity Foundation (MA)
- Verizon Foundation (NJ)
- Pfizer Foundation (NY)
- Batchelor Foundation (FL)
- Wells Fargo Foundation (CA)
- Goldman Sachs Foundation (NY)
- Capital Group Companies Charitable Foundation (CA)
- BP Foundation (IL)
- Abbott Fund (IL)

The Foundation Center has what I consider to be a very thorough and comprehensive listing of both electronic and print resources to inform the grant seeker regarding corporate giving. This information may be accessed at http:// www.foundationcenter.org/getstarted/faqs/html/corporate_giving.html. A number of print resources are listed. The site also mentions online resources such as Hoover's Online (http://www.hoovers.com/free), the Company/Executive Info section of David Lamb's Prospect Page, the Internet Prospectors' Reference Desk on Corporations (http://www.internetprospector.org), the Philanthropy News Digest (http://foundationcenter.org/pnd), and the Foundation Center's RFP Bulletin (http://foundationcenter.org/pnd/rfp/).

The Grantsmanship Center also offers information on corporate funding. The grant seeker may receive the names of corporate grant makers and the cities in which they are located at no charge. More detailed information on the 2,200 grant makers in the database is available for a fee on what is referred to as "Grant Domain," mentioned previously. This information includes areas of interest, full contact information, history, geographic areas served, the type of approach desired, and other pertinent information.

SERVICE CLUBS AND ORGANIZATIONS

Service clubs and organizations are among the most reliable sources of funding for local projects. Many of these organizations are part of a national organization that may fund specific types of activities consistent with their philosophy, orientation, and interests. These clubs may be service-oriented or fraternal organizations or both. The following entities may be able to provide a list of the service clubs in your area:

- local libraries
- chambers of Commerce
- municipal or county government
- news media

Service clubs vary widely in the source of their revenue and the amount that they have available to give. In several counties in my area, fraternal and service organizations are permitted by the state to have slot machines. However, this comes with the caveat that a certain percentage of the revenues realized through the slots will be donated to charity.

Most of these clubs appoint a committee to oversee the grant process and review requests periodically. It would therefore behoove the grant seeker to determine who the chairman of the grant committee is and make their approach to that person. I have seen a number of instances where a letter requesting funds is sent to the organization as a whole but not to the attention of any particular person. These requests generally are either lost or sit on someone's desk for a long time. It helps a great deal if someone on the grant committee is already familiar with your organization and knows your work. It is rare that a service club will request more than a simple letter. Most groups try to keep the process as uncomplicated as possible.

Once again, I recommend that the grant seeker contact as many service clubs as possible in order to maximize the chances of receiving funding. The same letter could be sent to all the organizations with only minor modifications.

Chapter Five

Search Advice for Specific Professions

LAW ENFORCEMENT

There are many sources of funds for law enforcement agencies for such purposes as the hiring of new employees, overtime, and the purchase of equipment. A significant portion of the funding available to law enforcement agencies is passed from the federal government to the states for distribution to local police departments and sheriffs' departments. In addition, many states appropriate funds from their own budget for this purpose. Generally, one agency plays the lead role in distributing the NOFA (Notice of Funding Availability) and accepting and reviewing applications.

In order to determine the agency that handles the funding for law enforcement in your state, go to the Web site for that state. Do a search for the state agency that handles law enforcement issues. In most cases, that is the agency that distributes the grant funds. In the state of Maryland, this agency is referred to as the Governor's Office of Crime Control and Prevention. However, in New Hampshire, for example, the appropriate agency is referred to as the Department of Safety. In Nevada, the administering agency for law enforcement grants is the Department of Public Safety.

The single largest source of law enforcement funds is the U.S. Department of Justice (DOJ). There are a number of programs administered by this agency that are channeled directly to local law enforcement agencies. A significant portion of the funds, however, are channeled to the states for distribution.

There are three separate categories of grants awarded by the DOJ to localities. One of these is the Community Oriented Policing Services (COPS) grants. This funding was created by the Violent Crime Control and Law Enforcement Act of 1994. The theory behind this program is that crime can be reduced by having law enforcement interact with the community through special events and neighborhood-oriented patrols. This program also recognizes that such activities as Neighborhood Watch, Operation ID, and D.A.R.E. (Drug Awareness and Resistance Education) can have a significant impact on reducing the crime rate.

Neighborhood Watch is, as its name implies, a neighborhood-based group of citizens that organize themselves to watch for suspicious activity. Operation ID offers citizens the benefit of having valuable personal possessions engraved with identifying information so that these possessions can easily be returned to the owners in the event of theft. D.A.R.E. teaches schoolchildren to avoid drug use. These and other community policing activities help law enforcement to address the root causes of crime. Since 1994, the COPS program has paid for 117,000 new officer positions and given out $12.4 billion.

The funding for COPS programs was at a reduced level during the period from 2005 to 2008. With the passage of the American Recovery and Reinvestment Act (ARRA) in February of 2009, additional funds were made available for COPS grants. Applications were accepted until April of 2009 for funding under the COPS Hiring Recovery Program. Funding was set aside to support 5,500 new sworn officer positions. Funds were made available for either the creation of a new position or the retention of a position that would have been eliminated due to the poor state of the nation's economy.

Other programs funded by COPS include: Cops in Schools, Secure Our Schools, Tribal Resources Grant Program, the Universal Hiring Program, the Child Sexual Predator Program, the Methamphetamine Initiative, the Technology Initiative Program, and a scholarship program to allow officers to attend the National Center for Victims of Crime conference. Complete information on COPS funding can be found at http://www.cops.usdoj.gov. Most of the COPS programs require that the application be submitted online through the Grants Management System (GMS) managed by the Justice Department.

The second category of Justice Department funding for law enforcement is handled through the Bureau of Justice Assistance (BJA). Information on these programs can be found at http://www.ojp.usdoj.gov/BJA. This office administers the well-known Edward Byrne Memorial Justice Assistance Grant, more commonly referred to as JAG. This program is named after a young law enforcement officer, Edward Byrne, who was killed at the age of 22 in the line of duty in 1988 while protecting a witness in a drug case in New York City.

JAG funds have recently been divided into four separate allocations. One goes to the various states for distribution to localities as well as for statewide use. A second allocation is given on a formula basis to law enforcement agencies across the country based on their crime statistics. The third allocation is made available to localities on a competitive basis. The final allocation was made available under the ARRA in the spring of 2009.

BJA gives a significant amount of attention to the problems and challenges of rural law enforcement agencies. For example, ARRA funds were made available to purchase equipment, pay for overtime, and create new positions through several subprograms under the Assistance to Rural Law Enforcement initiative. Some of BJA's other programs include the following: Citizen Corps, Mental Health Courts Program, Project Safe Neighborhoods, and the State Criminal Alien Assistance Program. The programs of BJA generally invite applications for each program once a year. The law enforcement grant administrator would be well advised to check both the COPS and BJA Web sites at least once every two weeks in order to determine what current solicitations might be applicable to his agency. Many of these applications must be submitted online through GMS. Agencies are required to register to submit applications and reports through the system.

Finally, the Justice Department makes grants available to local law enforcement agencies to pay 50 percent of the cost of bulletproof vests. This program, called the Bulletproof Vest Partnership Program, is open for applications once every year, generally in the spring. The application is submitted online and is quite simple to complete. Requests for payment for approved grants are also submitted online. Grantees have four years from the time of approval to expend the funds. Information on this program may be found at http://www.ojp.usdoj.gov/bvpbasi/.

The Federal Emergency Management Agency (FEMA) contributes equipment to law enforcement agencies and fire departments through its Commercial Equipment Direct Assistance Program (CEDAP). Information on this program can be found at https://www.rkb.us. Application periods are generally unpredictable. When the program was initiated in 2005, applications were solicited twice a year. This then went to once a year. However, no applications were solicited for 2009. Instead of making grants of cash to purchase equipment, CEDAP publishes a list of equipment it will furnish to successful applicants who must specify in the application one item they would find the most useful. CEDAP then either ships this equipment directly to the successful applicant or requires that personnel from that agency attend a training session and receive the equipment there.

The Community Facilities Program, administered by the U.S. Department of Agriculture (USDA), provides up to $50,000 in grant funding for law enforcement equipment. This includes the purchase of vehicles. The two current priorities under this program are health care and public safety, so law enforcement agencies are well-positioned to receive these funds. Loan funding at low interest rates is also available. These applications are accepted on a continuing basis, with no specific deadlines. Agencies must first submit a preapplication. If USDA is interested in the project, a full application is invited. This program is only available to communities with populations of 20,000 or less.

The National Tactical Officers Association (http://site.ntoa.org) of Doylestown, Pennsylvania, makes direct grants of equipment to law enforcement agencies who are members of the organization. The membership fee is relatively inexpensive and must be renewed on a yearly basis. This organization also offers a magazine, *The Tactical Edge,* and conducts an inexpensive tactical training program. The grant solicitations are generally offered at least twice yearly. Each piece of equipment is featured on the Web site, along with its respective application form and the number of each type of equipment that will be given to successful applicants. Typically, this program is extremely competitive, often with less than half a dozen of each item of equipment being given in this nationwide competition. The quality of the narrative is a key factor in receiving an award, but the organization also looks at the statistical data submitted. Although this program is very competitive, the applications are very brief and relatively easy to complete.

FIRE DEPARTMENTS

There are generally not as many sources of assistance for fire departments as there are for law enforcement agencies. Many of the volunteer departments in the country depend heavily on fund raising in the local community through fund drives, dinners, raffles, and other types of creative projects.

Fire departments are also eligible for the CEDAP program, mentioned in the previous section on law enforcement funding. However, that program is most definitely oriented toward law enforcement agencies. It is not that law enforcement is given preference in the rating and ranking, but it is that the equipment that is offered is generally more useful to law enforcement. However, because the application is relatively brief, it is worthwhile to apply.

The major federal program available for fire departments is the Assistance to Firefighters Grant (AFG) Program, which is administered by FEMA. While not completely open-ended as to what types of projects may be funded, a wide variety of activities are permissible. Departments may apply for funding to purchase equipment, vehicles, and personal protective equipment. If a department wishes to apply for funding to purchase a vehicle, it must submit a separate application for that vehicle and another application for any equipment that is desired. Applications are generally accepted once per year, usually in the spring. The interesting thing about this program is that not all of the award announcements are made at one time. FEMA makes awards right up to the time that the next year's solicitation opens.

The application must be submitted online. A great deal of basic information about the department is requested. This includes, among other things, contact information, call volume, characteristics of the area covered, inventory of vehicles, number of firefighter and civilian deaths and injuries, and budgetary information. The narrative is generally considered to be the most important part of the application and is limited to five pages.

The Assistance to Firefighters Grant Program also awards funding through two specialized grant programs. These are SAFER (Staffing for Adequate Fire and Emergency Response) and Fire Prevention and Safety Grants. Both, like the basic AFG program, accept applications only once a year. These applications must also be submitted online and are very similar to the basic AFG application. SAFER provides funds to enable fire departments to increase their staffing and capability to comply with the standards established by the National Fire Protection Association (NFPA) and the Occupational Safety and Health Administration (OSHA). One of the major goals of this program is to decrease response time and to raise the level of training within a particular department. Specifically, SAFER is more likely to fund projects that ensure that a minimum of four firefighters are trained to meet the standards of OSHA.

The Fire Prevention and Safety Grants are, for the most part, directed toward those communities with populations at high risk of death or injury from fires. Funds may be used to pay for fire prevention activities, media campaigns, arson prevention and awareness programs, and research and development.

In July of 2009, the AFG program offered a one-time solicitation for funding to construct new firehouses or rehabilitate existing ones so that fire departments may better serve their communities. This program was funded with ARRA monies. Information regarding all of the aforementioned FEMA grants may be accessed at http://www.fema.gov.

The USDA Community Facilities Program is also a possibility for fire departments. This program, mentioned in the previous section for law enforcement agencies, accepts applications on a continuous basis. A number of fire departments have utilized this program to construct new firehouses. This is one of the very few programs that will fund new construction for fire departments. Again, this program is only available to assist in communities with populations of 20,000 or less.

The USDA has a second program that funds projects undertaken by fire departments. This is called the Fire and Rescue Program (FRP). Again, applications are accepted on a year-round basis. The application itself is rather lengthy. The FRP provides loans and grants to nonprofit organizations, associations, and cooperatives for the purchases of major equipment and construction of buildings. The Rural Development Administration, a division of USDA, administers this program, as well as the Community Facilities

Program. These programs also guarantee loans made by other lenders. The purchase of vehicles and professional fees associated with the development of a new building are also eligible costs. The Rural Development Administration reviews the applications in order to determine whether the applicant is unable to obtain the funds from other sources at reasonable rates and terms. The agency also is looking for organizations that are financially sound and that are able to organize and manage the project effectively.

Most states give some form of assistance to fire departments and rescue companies. The agencies administering these funds vary from state to state. However, fire department grant seekers are urged to check their state emergency management agency as well as the state department that deals with natural resources. In some cases, the natural resources state agencies will provide funding for equipment that will assist fire departments in fighting forest fires. Many county governments also give regular yearly allocations to local fire departments.

Fire departments are also eligible for funding from many local foundations. It is suggested that departments contact each such foundation for their guidelines and check to see whether their organization would be eligible for assistance. Quite often, many local foundations give to a wide range of causes, unlike many statewide and national foundations, which give only to certain very narrowly focused areas of interest.

ECONOMIC DEVELOPMENT

In general, most economic development organizations are part of municipal, county, or state governments. In some cases, such organizations are independent but have local elected officials as board members. Many of the most effective economic development organizations are those that cover several political jurisdictions—that is, multiple counties. These entities have a strategic advantage in grant seeking due to the fact that state and federal funding sources generally prefer a collaborative effort. The reason for this is that generally such projects can exhibit a greater benefit and public purpose.

The USDA's Rural Development Administration offers several programs that benefit economic development efforts. One of the most popular is the Rural Business Enterprise Grant (RBEG). This program was designed to assist "small and emerging businesses" in rural areas with populations of less than 50,000. However, priority is given to those communities and areas with a population less than 25,000.

Small and emerging business is defined as any enterprise with 50 or fewer employees and less than $1 million in gross revenues. Applications are accepted on a continuing basis. Funds have been used to create revolving loan funds that are under the control of a local government, which is then free to create its own guidelines within certain parameters. The grantees must ensure that the loan program provides optimal benefit to the businesses that borrow from it and serves a public purpose, such as job creation and/or an increase in the tax base. These funds may also be used to pay for infrastructure such as water and sewer or streets in support of new businesses that may be moving into the area. Projects given a high priority by USDA are those that create a significant number of jobs or that may introduce a new technology or industry into an area. Information about this program may be found at http://www.rurdev.usda.gov/rbs/busp/rbeg.htm.

Another USDA program that provides funding for revolving loan funds is the Intermediary Re-lending Program. This is very similar to RBEG in its requirements and application forms. There are no specific deadlines for application submission. The small businesses that become the borrowers may receive up to $250,000 in loans. Individuals may borrow funds from the intermediary.

The entire listing of business programs available from the USDA Rural Development Administration can be found at http://www.rurdev.usda.gov/rbs/busp/bprogs.htm. The programs not specifically discussed here fund rural utilities, including electric coops; telemedicine; broadband; sustainable energy; and a wide variety of other projects.

The other federal agency that gives a substantial amount of funding for economic development projects is the Economic Development Administration (EDA) of the U.S. Department of Commerce. One of the major thrusts of EDA funding is public works projects in support of new commercial and industrial development that creates a substantial number of new jobs. In fact, the "name of the game" at EDA is "jobs, jobs, and more jobs!" The agency is interested both in projects that create new jobs as well as those that retain jobs that are in danger of being lost. Grants are generally made for up to 50 percent or more of the project cost, although EDA may contribute a higher percentage if an area is experiencing severe economic distress. EDA is particularly interested in projects that have a regional focus, overlapping state boundaries. Examples of projects funded include construction of broadband service and infrastructure for industrial parks such as water and sewer service, roads, and storm drainage. Grants are also made for planning and technical assistance projects. Local governments and regional planning organizations are eligible to apply.

The grant writer is strongly advised to discuss the project with EDA staff in the regional office serving her geographic area. Grant funding of greater than 50 percent is provided to those areas considered to be economically distressed. Criteria for economic distress include a high unemployment rate; a low per capita income; or a special need such as substantial population loss, major natural disasters, closure of industrial firms essential to the area's economy, and the destructive impacts of foreign trade.

EDA makes funding in several areas including the following:

- Public Works and Economic Development Program—This program funds infrastructure in support of job creation and retention, such as water, sewer, and streets.
- Economic Adjustment Assistance Program—This involves assistance given to regions having economic challenges. This assistance may be in the form of infrastructure construction, planning, or technical assistance.
- Research and National Technical Assistance—provides funding for research in regard to economic development best practices that can be applied on a national or international level.
- Local Technical Assistance—As its name implies, EDA assists local and nonprofit sectors in economically distressed regions to implement viable and successful economic development strategies.
- Planning Program—Under this program, assistance is given to local planning organizations in the development of their Comprehensive Economic Development Strategy (CEDS). This is discussed in more detail below.
- University Center Economic Development Program—This program promotes a partnership between the federal government and various universities so that the resources of these institutions of higher learning are available to local governments and organizations that need assistance with economic development.
- Trade Adjustment Assistance for Firms Program—This program assists firms that have lost business due to an increase in imports. The service is provided by eleven Trade Adjustment Assistance Centers around the country. The goal is to help these firms become more competitive in the global economy.
- Global Climate Change Mitigation Incentive Fund—This program was established to strengthen the linkages between economic development and environmental quality. The purpose and mission of the GCCMIF is to finance projects that foster economic development by advancing the green economy in distressed communities.

An area may apply for designation as an Economic Development District. The advantage of this designation is that any subsequent applications requesting assistance for public works projects may receive an additional 10 percent in EDA grant assistance.

The EDA process, in all honesty, is lengthy and complex. The application requires a significant investment of time. However, the part of the process that requires the most substantial amount of money and staff time is the development of a Comprehensive Economic Development Strategy. This is a very detailed planning document that describes the assets and challenges of an area; outlines specific goals and objectives; and describes in detail the specific projects designed to alleviate economic distress, including the time-frame in which these projects will be implemented, the amount of funding needed, the source of that funding, and the responsible entity.

For smaller jurisdictions, it is unlikely that existing staff would have either the time or the expertise to develop a CEDS. There are consultants who specialize in this type of work. However, even when a consultant is hired, the staff time required to support the consultant is considerable. Another factor that increases the amount of work and time put into a plan is the requirement that a committee representing a broad cross-section of the private and public sectors must be involved in the development of the plan. This document must be updated regularly for the jurisdiction to continue to be eligible for EDA funds. In the final analysis, the time and money spent to develop a CEDS is well worth it if the community wishes to receive EDA funding for large projects. More detailed information on EDA programs is available at http://www.eda.gov.

EDA has done an excellent job of listing other resources for economic development on this Web site. These resources include both funding and technical assistance. The grant seeker should click on "Resources" on the main EDA Web page. This will open up a very helpful listing of organizations and government entities that will assist in this effort. One of the most valuable is the listing of state and local economic development offices. Each state is represented on this listing. In many cases, the link will take the grant seeker directly to the agency within that state that deals with economic development grants. In some cases, however, the link will take the reader to the state's general Web site. When that occurs, it is necessary to scroll down the list of various state agencies in order to find the one whose name intuitively implies that its purpose is to promote economic development.

Other resources shown on this site are the following: Trade Adjustment Assistance Centers, University Centers, federal agencies in partnership with EDA, economic development foundations, national economic development organizations; and Economic Development Districts. The page dealing with economic development foundations is merely a searchable database of foundations in general. The researcher will need to specify the words "economic development" in the search. This is not a listing of foundations that only fund economic development projects.

Another federal agency that works to promote economic development is the Small Business Administration (SBA). However, most of their programs are geared to assist individual small businesses. Because the thrust of this section is to primarily help local governments and regional planning organizations, SBA programs will be discussed in the section dealing with funding assistance for individuals and small businesses.

The Small Cities Community Development Block Grant (CDBG) Program is a very versatile and popular program that funds a variety of economic development projects throughout the country. Although each state has the latitude to administer certain parts of the program in its own fashion, a significant portion of the regulations and procedures are dictated by the federal government. The grant seeker should contact the state agency involved in administering these funds. In many cases, this would be the same agency that handles the state economic development funding programs (see previous description of EDA programs). The appropriate state office will be able to let the grant seeker know whether they accept these applications on a continuous basis throughout the year or whether there are one or more application cycles with a specific due date.

One of the major goals of this program is to create or retain jobs. A secondary goal is to eliminate or prevent slums or blight. CDBG funds may only be granted directly to a municipality or county or a combination of local jurisdictions. These local jurisdictions may use the funds in direct support of private enterprise in several ways. Water, sewer, streets, or storm drainage may be improved or constructed in order to serve a new business or retain an existing business. In this case, the grantee (the local jurisdiction) would remain the owner of the infrastructure. Assistance may also be given to improve or construct a physical building that will house a new business, defray demolition costs, or to purchase land. In certain cases, these activities improve the property of a private business. Generally, the state CDBG staff works with the applicant to determine whether this assistance can be given in the form of a grant (this is rare and done generally where the amount of CDBG assistance is very small compared to the private investment) or a low-interest loan.

There are very strict rules regarding documentation to prove that the jobs benefit actually occurred. It is a condition of the grant award that at least 51 percent of the jobs created or retained must be taken by or made available to low- and moderate-income persons. The specific income levels for this category change from year to year and from geographic area to geographic area. HUD generally publishes the new income levels every spring. Businesses that are beneficiaries of this assistance must keep records regarding each employee to show that they have met the conditions for the grant. This information includes income prior to taking the job, household size, gender, and disability status. It is very important to impress upon businesses that this is a condition of the assistance and that certain sanctions can be applied if the requested information is not given. There have been cases where businesses cooperate until the funding has actually been expended on their project, but then suppress this information or fail to keep it afterwards.

There are a number of very involved administrative requirements, so it is well to engage the services of someone who is familiar with this program. There is a rather complex environmental review process, specific financial recordkeeping requirements, and labor standards to be followed. The latter includes checking to see that federal wage rates are followed and that local suppliers and subcontractors are engaged wherever possible. The contractor is also charged with attempting to engage Disadvantaged Business Enterprise (DBE) participation. DBEs can be minority- or female-owned businesses or any other type of enterprise that has historically experienced difficulty in the marketplace due to discrimination or an economic disadvantage.

The competition for these funds is generally very intense. It is essential to let the granting agency know that the program will be administered properly and that the required documentation on job creation or retention will be obtained. CDBG funds are more likely to be granted in areas that are experiencing economic distress.

At this point, it is very important that the grant seeker know that state economic development funds are critically important and should be pursued vigorously. Obviously, it is impossible to discuss the economic development funds available from each state, and so I have primarily focused upon federal programs in this section. I actually look first at state programs to fund economic development activities, due to the lower level of competition as compared to federal programs.

For example, Maryland provides funding for downtown revitalization activities that can benefit private businesses. This can include façade improvement of commercial buildings in a downtown area. Some of the assistance given by the state is in the form of equity investment for the aquaculture, information technology, and life sciences sectors. These funds are made available as "seed" or starting money. Other types of assistance given by the state of Maryland include the issuance of revenue bonds, credit insurance, and direct loans and guarantees. Special attention is given to the modernization of manufacturing techniques, the development of commercial applications for technology, assistance to businesses that cannot qualify for conventional financing, and assistance to businesses owned by persons who have been historically disadvantaged. I am giving this information to use my state as an example of the diversity of economic development assistance available at the state level. I strongly urge the grant seeker to search for state funds for this purpose.

HERITAGE TOURISM AND HISTORIC PRESERVATION

One of the most effective programs in this area is the National Scenic Byways Program. The U.S. Department of Transportation administers this program through the Federal Highway Administration (FHA), but it delegates certain duties to the states, which nearly always handle this through their own departments of transportation. Two types of assistance are available. Local heritage organizations and local governments may apply for the designation of heritage routes within their jurisdiction as either National Scenic Byways or State Scenic Byways. Obviously, the national status confers a greater degree of benefits. The main advantage is the promotion and marketing undertaken by the federal government or the states, depending on which designation has been given. Applications for National Scenic Byways status are only accepted every few years.

The National Scenic Byways Program also awards grant funds for various activities undertaken by approved byway organizations to promote the byway and attract additional visitors. This could include signage, planning, the development of brochures and other marketing materials, the development of media materials, and other projects intended to make the byway more attractive and more easily accessible. Applications must be submitted online and are solicited once a year, with a preapplication and an application. State staff reviews each application and sends it on with recommendations to FHA. Information regarding the National Scenic Byways Program may be accessed at http://www.byways.org.

Having a Corridor Management Plan is a requirement to access certain types of funding from this agency. This detailed planning document should discuss the various attractions and challenges along the route and offer a strategy for maximizing the appeal of the byway and attracting additional visitors.

The Preserve America initiative provides designations to communities that operate exemplary historic preservation programs. Preserve America communities can be municipalities, counties, or neighborhoods within large cities. These communities are eligible to apply for grant funding that focuses on planning and the development of sustainable management strategies. The program aims to provide management capabilities that will ensure that these assets are federally protected from having their integrity compromised in any way and that they are maintained properly. Grant amounts range from $20,000–$250,000. In general, applications for grant funds are solicited once a year. Applications to receive designation as a Preserve America community are solicited quarterly. This designation provides more than just the eligibility to apply for grant funds. Designated communities receive a Preserve America Community road sign, authorization to use the Preserve America logo, and marketing of their community at the federal level.

The Advisory Council on Historic Preservation plays a lead role in administering this program. However, a number of federal agencies are represented on the steering committee. Visit http://www.preserveamerica.gov to learn more about this program.

Save America's Treasures (SAT) is another federal program that provides funding to assist in heritage tourism and historic preservation. SAT is administered by the National Park Service with input from the National Endowment for the Arts, the National Endowment for the Humanities, the Institute of Museum and Library Services, and the Presidential Commission on Arts and Humanities. The National Trust for Historic Preservation is a partner in the sense that it works with SAT grantees in order to locate the required matching funds.

This program only makes grants for two purposes. Funding is provided to preserve nationally significant intellectual and cultural artifacts and to preserve nationally significant historical buildings and sites. In the case of artifacts, the applicant is given the opportunity to make the case for national significance. In the case of historic properties, funds are only awarded to assist in the preservation of sites that have been designated as a National Historic Landmark, that are contributing structures in a National Historic Landmark District, or that are on the National Register of Historic Places due to their national significance. Applications are solicited once a year. A maximum of $700,000 per project is granted. The grant must be matched by an equal amount of funding from other sources. Eligible applicants are governmental agencies and nonprofits. For more information on this program, go to http://www.saveamericastreasures.org.

The National Park Service administers a number of other programs that are described more fully at http://www.nps.gov/history/grants.htm. There are specific programs directed toward the preservation of battlefields; historic buildings located on the campuses of historically black colleges and universities; Japanese American confinement sites; Native American graves and repatriation sites; and tribal heritage. Grants for preservation planning are made available to nonprofits, universities, and federal agencies.

The National Center for Preservation Technology and Training (http://www.ncptt.nps.gov) is a separate office within the National Park Service. This agency works to promote the application of science and technology to historic preservation. Grants are accepted once a year, usually in late summer. The maximum amount of funding awarded to any one project is $25,000. The Web site states that, "grants are made to fund the agency's research priorities: protecting cultural resources against vandalism, looting, terrorism and natural disasters; conserving architectural materials of the recent past; developing appropriate technologies to preserve houses of worship and cemeteries; monitoring and evaluating preservation treatments; studying environmental effects of pollution on cultural resources; and documenting and preserving threatened cultural landscapes."

The National Endowment for the Arts (http://www.nea.gov) is another source of funding for cultural and heritage projects. The endowment supports local projects and contributes to the state arts councils. Support is given for museums as well as the performing arts and projects aimed at preserving the folk life of a particular group or area. Three of the major programs are as follows: Access to Artistic Excellence, which funds projects aimed at improving public access to the arts, museums, and other heritage resources; Challenge America Reaching Every Community Fast-Track Review Grants, aimed at improving the access of underserved communities to the arts; and the Learning in the Arts for Children and Youth, which, as its name implies, serves to fund projects that increase the access of young people to arts projects. Applications are solicited once or twice per year. Grant amounts generally range between $5,000 and $150,000.

The National Endowment for the Humanities (http://www.neh.gov) accepts applications once a year for several programs designed to encourage the development of humanities programs and to preserve collections. The term *humanities* includes heritage tourism, historic preservation, folk culture, and museum programs. Most of the grants are given on a challenge basis, with the grantee being required to raise three times the amount of the federal grant in many, but not all, cases. Applications are accepted once a year for the regular Challenge Grant Program and the We the People Challenge Grant. The latter makes grants only to organizations working with projects that have a national significance.

The Institute of Museum and Library Services (http://www.imls.gov), as its name implies, supports only museums and libraries. One of its major programs is the Museum Assessment Program, which provides resources to help museums evaluate their operations. Other assistance programs include Museums for America, National Leadership Grants, Native American Library Services, and Native Hawaiian Library Services.

The National Trust for Historic Preservation, a private organization located in Washington, D.C., also offers a number of grants directed toward heritage tourism and historic preservation projects. Its Web site, http://www. preservationnation.org, describes several programs directed at specific areas of historic preservation.

The National Trust Preservation Fund provides matching grants of from $500 to $5,000 for preservation planning and education. Funding is also provided for preservation emergencies. Examples of preservation planning activities may include the services of experts in architecture, archaeology, engineering, preservation planning, land use planning, fundraising, and organizational development.

The Johanna Favrot Fund for Historic Preservation provides grants for professional advice, conferences, workshops, and education programs that contribute "to the preservation or the recapture of an authentic sense of space," as stated on the Web site. Prospective grantees must in general apply for at least $2,500 and no more than $10,000. There are some exceptions to this. Nonprofits and governmental entities may apply for funding for any type of project that meets these general guidelines. Individuals and for-profit businesses may apply only if the project for which funding is requested involves a National Historic Landmark.

The Cynthia Woods Mitchell Fund for Historic Interiors is concerned with preserving the inside of historic buildings. Again, grants range from

$2,500 to $10,000. Eligible applicants are the same as those stated for the Johanna Favrot Fund.

Heritage Preservation (http://www.heritagepreservation.org), a national nonprofit, whose mission is to assist museums, provides assistance worth $3,000–$6,500 to undertake conservation assessments. This funding is geared toward any nonprofit institution that possesses a collection of items that tells a story. This could include museums as well as zoos, botanical gardens, and historical houses. The collection must be small enough to be surveyed within two days. The site also lists other sources for historical conservation.

Tourism Cares for Tomorrow (http://www.tourismcares.org) is a national nonprofit organization that promotes tourism and provides resources for both capital and educational projects operated by local nonprofits. Potential applicants must first submit a letter of inquiry. Those projects needing the qualifications and guidelines of Tourism Cares for Tomorrow are then invited to submit a full proposal. Grants of up to $10,000 are distributed in two solicitations per year. Preference is given to those projects that have secured matching funds, those that are supported by the local community, and those that are endorsed by tourism offices.

There are significant resources available for historic preservation and heritage tourism at the state level. Nearly every state has its own arts council, many of which offer grant programs. Check http://www.nasaa-arts.org, the Web site of the National Assembly of State Arts Agencies, for contact information for each state arts council.

Likewise, there are 56 state and territorial humanities councils. These agencies provide funding to local governments and nonprofits for a wide array of heritage projects. The humanities councils are funded in part by the National Endowment for the Humanities. A complete listing of these organizations can be found at http://www.neh.gov/whoweare/StateCouncils.html.

Each state also has its own State Historic Preservation Organization, or SHPO. The Web site http://www.ncshpo.org gives the contact information for the SHPO in each state. These agencies administer the federal tax credits for historic preservation that originate with the U.S. Department of the Interior, along with other, state-funded programs. The federal tax credits amount to 20 percent of the cost of rehabilitation. This program is administered by the National Park Service and the Internal Revenue Service in conjunction with the SHPO. The tax credit is available only for commercial, industrial, agricultural or rental residential income-producing properties. If a portion of one's residence is used for business, the rehabilitation that applies to that portion of the home may be eligible for the tax credit. Eligible properties are located on the National Register of Historic Places or in a locally certified district or any historic district that is potentially eligible for the National Register. The federal government regulates the type of work that is done by requiring recipients of this tax credit to adhere to the Secretary of the Interior's standards for rehabilitation. The building must have retained its physical integrity prior to rehabilitation.

The James Marston Fitch Charitable Foundation (http://www.fitchfoun dation.org) located in New York, New York, gives grants of up to $25,000 to midcareer professionals with established credentials in historic preservation, architecture, urban planning, and related fields.

WATER AND SEWER

Virtually all of the funding available for water and sewer projects is provided by federal and state governmental agencies. In most cases, these projects are owned and operated by municipal or county governments. There are only a few sources of funding for this type of project. Federal sources are the USDA Rural Development Administration, the Environmental Protection Agency (EPA), and the CDBG.

Nearly every state has an agency charged with regulating the water and sewer systems of the localities within that state. Most of these agencies administer funding for the localities. The best way to find the appropriate agency in your state is to get on the state Web site and select an agency whose title indicates that this is its purpose. If this does not work, call the Governor's office. An examination of the Web site will contain information on funding programs. Some of the funding administered by each state comes from the EPA, while some comes from the state itself.

The Rural Development Administration is responsible for administering the Water and Waste Program. These funds are only distributed to communities in rural areas with a population of less than 10,000. Solid waste projects are eligible for assistance as well. Up to 100 percent of project costs may be paid. However, grant funds may comprise no more than 75 percent of the total project cost up to a maximum of $4 million. The remaining 25 percent is provided as a loan. Both public agencies and nonprofits are eligible to apply. The funds may be utilized for land acquisition, construction, engineering, equipment, and administration. A preapplication, which includes an environmental report, is the first step in the application process. Applicants deal with the appropriate regional office. USDA staff inspects the project several times while it is under construction.

The EPA (http://www.epa.gov) also awards funds for water and sewer projects through its regional offices. The program that is utilized quite often is the Special Appropriations Program. These funds are most commonly accessed by having the applicant's U.S. Senator or Congressman initiate the process. I have seen instances where my clients have received a communication from one of our senators with no warning whatsoever that they were eligible for Special Appropriations funding. In other instances, the community or nonprofit will contact their congressional representatives asking them to include their project in that year's appropriation. The applicants must still file the appropriate application, which is relatively simple to prepare. EPA funds are generally administered by the state agency that regulates water and sewer. These agencies are responsible for inspection and approval of payment requests.

There are a number of limitations on the use of CDBG funds for water and sewer projects. This program requires that 51 percent of the beneficiaries of any funded projects must be of low- and moderate-income status, as defined by income guidelines published each year by the U.S. Department of Housing and Urban Development. That agency compiles this information at the local level. Many water and sewer projects have a community-wide scope. Therefore, the citizens of a community that wishes to use these funds for this type of project must be predominantly low- and moderate-income. This data is kept by the state agency that is charged with administering the program.

If a community does not qualify under the low- and moderate-income criterion, but feels that recent changes in the demographics and income level of its residents have changed since the last Census was published, it may conduct an income survey.

Obviously, this is easier in a small community. Generally, a minimum percentage of responses must be received in order to meet the guidelines for income surveys. Households are mailed survey forms that request information on the size of the household. A range of incomes is then given. The residents may indicate which range applies to them. Therefore, the individual households are not required to give their exact income. Quite often, it is necessary to follow up with telephone calls and visits, as the return rate by mail may be 50 percent or less. Income surveys are also used in cases where a water and sewer project will benefit only one particular neighborhood. In this case, surveys are only sent to those households in that neighborhood.

Water and sewer projects funded by CDBG must either be relatively small in scope or must have matching funds from other agencies. Many communities use this program to pay the costs of hook-ups to water and sewer service for lower-income neighborhoods. In this case, an income survey is required to establish that that particular neighborhood meets the income limits. Once the grant is approved, however, the grantee municipality or county must individually qualify individual households receiving assistance. In most cases, a simple application form is used for this purpose. Families must submit proof of income in order to qualify.

INDIVIDUALS

I have found this to be a topic of immense interest in today's world. I have had an unprecedented number of inquiries from individuals just in the past year. Perhaps this is because more people are daring to "dream their dream" and want to find ways to live it. I think that we as a society are beginning to see more avenues for individual expression. There seems to be a feeling that all things are possible and that the sky is the limit. I see this as a very beneficial thing. However, the grant world has not yet caught up with this new trend. Grant opportunities for individuals are very few in number.

On the face of it, this is probably because funding agencies feel that making grants to individuals raises a heightened risk of funds being misappropriated. The lack of financial controls and checks and balances in this type of situation has caused grant makers to become somewhat nervous and leery. I can well understand this.

The vast majority of grants available in this category come in the form of scholarships or fellowships. A significant portion of the remaining grants is given to researchers who often must be affiliated with a university or other research institution in order to qualify for funds. The only way that requirement can be avoided would be if the researcher was of such significant standing that this affiliation was considered unnecessary.

Most of the grants remaining after scholarships, fellowships, and research grants are deducted from the equation are given to support creative projects, primarily in the arts or in writing. It is very difficult to take the time to write or create art while working full time. However, most individuals undertaking this type of work are forced to fit it in around other obligations, which include making a living. Of course, there are the lucky few who are able to support themselves in this fashion once they become established. I once talked to an author who had written a book that was quite popular in certain circles. He was interested in finding a source of income to support him while he was writing the second book, as he was finding it almost impossible to juggle the intense research schedule for the book with another job. Despite an exhaustive search, he was unable to find a grant to help him. This example shows the scarcity of support for talented, creative individuals.

There are two very simple ways to check the available grants for individuals. Grants.gov gives information on grants available to individuals from the federal agencies that participate in this initiative. The Foundation Center provides a reasonably priced subscription to an online database that deals only with grants to individuals. I am unaware of any search mechanism that tracks state grants for individuals. In this case, the applicant would have to go his or her state Web site and review the guidelines for every grant that looks as if it would be suitable for the activity in question.

In order to find grants for individuals on Grants.gov, go to the Web site (http://www.grants.gov) and click on "Find Grant Opportunities" on the left-hand side of the home page. At that point, click on "Advanced Search" and search by applicant eligibility. One of the choices here is "individual." The searcher can further narrow the request by specifying either open opportunities, closed opportunities, or archived opportunities. One of the reasons to check closed and archived opportunities is to become aware of grant opportunities that may be available in the future. Many programs are only open for applications once a year. It is possible that a very promising program may have just closed the application period but will become available again. I would recommend that the individual interested in government grants check Grants.gov every two weeks or so. This is due to the fact that funding opportunities may be open for only a short time. The searcher may also specify the funding activity categories or funding type (grant, cooperative agreements, procurement contract, or other).

The individual seeker of grants from foundations may access the Foundation Center's database by going to http://foundationcenter.org/findfunders/fundingsources/gtio.html. The best bet is to purchase a one-month subscription for $19.95. Most people would be able to research and save information on opportunities of interest to them within the 30-day period. Other options are to purchase a three-month subscription for $36.95 or a one-year subscription for $99.95. Generally, the one-year subscription is most useful to organizations that counsel individuals on a continuous basis, such as university career centers.

This subscription will enable the individual to receive quarterly updates, daily search tips and links to free Web resources. There are a variety of search options, including the foundation city and state, the foundation name, the field of interest, geographic areas served, place of support, and a text search. Subscribers to the general database of foundations can also search for grants to individuals.

FOR-PROFIT BUSINESSES

Owners of for-profit businesses will benefit from reading the previous section on economic development. That section is written with an eye toward economic development professionals in the local government field. However, the information can assist a for-profit business in dealing with economic development offices. It is helpful to know what is available in the economic development professional's toolkit. I would particularly refer the business owner to the information regarding the CDBG program and the USDA.

This section, however, is written with the goal of assisting individual businesses in their own search for funds as opposed to looking at the broader picture of economic development in a particular city or county. I would strongly recommend that for-profit businesses approach the economic development offices in their area first. Many localities have programs that assist local business. Two examples of locally administered programs are facade improvement programs in downtowns and revolving loan funds. Most of the time, these programs are funded with monies from the federal or state government. Their goal is to improve local economic indicators, such as the unemployment rate and assessable base.

Economic development departments can also be extremely helpful to individual businesses in that most of them are the referral point for state and federal programs that can help them. Obviously, there is a variation in the services provided by different economic development offices depending on their budget and staffing. Most of these offices provide a complete referral service to local businesses and assist them throughout the entire process up to and including the submittal of the applications for assistance. Most of the time, these services are free.

If your city or county does not have an economic development office that assists local business, the next step would be to contact the state's economic development department. Most states have specific agencies dedicated to business development and administer financial assistance programs. The business owner would be well advised to either contact the relevant staff member or to search the Web site.

The major federal agency charged with assisting small business is the Small Business Administration (SBA; http://www.sba.gov). SBA provides help in the form of counseling, financial assistance, and expert advice regarding contracting opportunities with the federal government.

S.C.O.R.E. (Service Corps of Retired Executives) is a nonprofit organization that partners with SBA in order to provide free advice and low-cost workshops to small businesses. There are 364 chapters of this organization, which comprises working and retired business executives. Its name is therefore a bit misleading. The Web site can be found at http://www.score.org/index.html.

Small Business Development Centers throughout the country counsel small businesses on their management strategies. These centers are organized to provide for cooperation between the private sector; the educational community; and federal, state, and local governments. Women's Business Centers provide assistance to the female entrepreneur. SBA also provides help to businesses interested in going international.

SBA provides assistance to help small, disadvantaged, and female businesses receive federal government contracts. The agency has a program to provide surety bond guarantees. This helps contractors who cannot obtain bonding through regular channels. These bonds are required for many government-funded projects. If the contractor fails to complete the project, the surety bond will pay the project owner for the cost of the uncompleted work.

Venture capital is a type of private equity capital usually provided for companies that are just starting out and that have a lot of potential in exchange for shares in the company. It is provided through Small Business Investment Companies, which are privately owned and managed investment funds regulated by SBA. These companies are permitted to borrow funds at favorable rates from SBA in order to provide operating money.

Most of the financial programs provide loan guarantees. The agency's primary program is referred to as "7(a)." This program provides a guarantee to a bank loan that is structured to SBA requirements. Businesses may not participate in 7(a) if they have access to other borrowing at reasonable terms.

The Small Business Innovation Research (SBIR) program provides for-profit businesses with the opportunity to access a reserved portion of federal research and development funds. A company applies to become an SBIR firm on a competitive basis. Eleven federal departments participate in the program. In order to qualify, a firm must be American-owned, have less than 500 employees, be a for-profit concern, and have the principal researcher employed by that business. Funds are provided for the start-up and development phases.

The Small Business Technology Transfer (STTR) Program provides joint ventures involving small businesses and nonprofit research institutions with an opportunity to access a special reservation of federal funds. Five federal agencies participate in this program. This is done in recognition of the fact that small businesses often do not have access to research and nonprofit research institutions do not have the means to translate that research into commercial ventures. The qualifications for participating in this program are the same as the SBIR program except that the principal researcher need not be employed by the small business. The nonprofit research institution must be a federally funded research and development center.

Federal funding for small businesses may also be found at Grants.gov. In order to see the universe of grant opportunities available for small businesses (or businesses of any size) go to the site and only specify the type of applicant, leaving all other search fields blank. The searcher may specify one of the following: opportunities that are open to small businesses; those that are open to businesses that are not considered to be small; and those that are unrestricted, meaning that any type of entity may apply. Just to give the reader an example, I conducted this type of search on Grants.gov in late October of 2009. Of the total of 1,184 grant programs that were open for applications at that time, 647 were open to small businesses, 615 were open to businesses other than small concerns, and 165 were unrestricted.

Chapter Six

Evaluating Grant Sources and Developing a Strategy

EVALUATION PROCESS

Now that we have finished our research, it is time to put it all together and develop a strategy, or plan of action, by which we can access grant funds for our project. The most important rule to follow here, as stressed in the previous chapter, is to be inclusive when it comes to developing a list of potential funding sources. If there is any doubt at all, it is best to keep that source on the list. This is particularly true of private foundations where often the first inquiry is a two-page letter. In most cases, the same letter can be sent to multiple foundations with very slight variations. There is therefore little or no cost involved in including additional foundations on the "potentials" list. It is much better to include some sources that may not work rather than miss out on a source that might later prove to be a beautiful fit for the project.

Most governmental grant programs are generally rather clear in their guidelines. Once again, the idea here is to look for "deal breakers" such as project eligibility, applicant eligibility, geographical eligibility, due date, and matching funds. If there is any doubt at all, it is absolutely essential to contact the funding agency to get clarification. It makes no sense to commit significant staff resources to write an application only to have it be turned down during the initial review without being rated or ranked due to ineligibility. It can also be quite embarrassing to explain to your boss or to your Board of Directors.

Once the grant writer determines whether the project (or the applicant agency) will meet threshold (eligibility) review, it is time to determine the chances of success versus the staff resources required to complete the applications. There are several variables here, and the process somewhat resembles a juggling act. If the application is relatively simple, it makes sense to apply even if chances of getting the funding may not be the most promising. In this case, relatively few resources will be utilized, but yet there is still a chance of receiving grant money. There is no magic formula that tells you when the committal of resources is worth it. This is a highly personalized decision made by the applicant agency and will in part depend upon how ample the agency's resources are. If the organization is operating on a shoestring, it may not be worth the effort to have three staff members take two entire days to prepare an application that only has about a 10–15 percent chance of being funded. There are better ways to utilize staff resources.

On the other hand, an application with a relatively high chance of being funded should be submitted even if a significant amount of time and resources is involved. It is better to stretch oneself a bit and "go out on the limb" in order to have the best chance of succeeding at grant seeking. Even if the first try does not succeed, the organization is in a better position the following grant round and may very well receive the funds at that time. A resubmittal of the same application obviously does not involve nearly as much work. In addition, if your agency submits two or more of this type of application, even if the staff is hard-pressed for a short period of time, the odds are that you will receive approval for least one of these applications.

Most federal applications require a substantial amount of work. It is also well to keep in mind that federal programs are awarded through national competitions. It is a good idea to not apply to federal programs if the project is marginal and significant resources are needed to complete the application. For this reason, it may be well to give preference to state programs.

Other search criteria that can eliminate certain private foundations are geographic eligibility, eligibility of the applicant, and eligibility of the activity. The chances of receiving funds from a local foundation or from a foundation that only awards grants within a certain state are much higher than receiving funds from a foundation that gives on a national basis. The grant seeker is also advised to try to match its proposed project as closely as possible with the interest areas of the various foundations. A client recently asked me to search for funding to construct a building that would house a local Boy Scout troop. When searching foundations that give nationally, I only specified those that are interested in giving to Boy Scout projects. If I had searched for national foundations that are interested in giving to youth activities, the list would have been too long and it would have been very difficult to sort it out. However, in searching local and state foundations in my area, I included both areas of interest—Boy Scouts and youth. The advantage in applying to local and state foundations was enough to include those only stating an interest in youth activities.

When making telephone or e-mail inquiries to private foundations in order to determine the eligibility of your project for their funding, keep your questions short and direct. You will be much more likely to receive an answer this way. Do not ask them to make a detailed critique of your project's eligibility. They do not have the time for this.

One last word on eliminating various sources—clearly, those funding agencies whose applications and administrative requirements are beyond the scope of your ability should be taken off your list. One example that comes to mind is many of the programs funded by the National Institutes of Health (NIH). The majority of the funding awarded by this agency is for scientific research that must have a principal lead investigator with sufficient academic and research credentials. In addition, the project must be rigorously designed in order to follow the protocols accepted by the scientific community. The applications are extremely lengthy and complex and it is most helpful if a scientist completes the majority of the items. It is almost impossible to "get your foot in the door" unless you are a recognized academic/scientist/researcher. Several laypeople have approached me about applying to NIH for rather loosely organized studies dealing with mental and physical health. I have told all of them that such an application would be a waste of time. This is something that I very seldom tell anyone.

DEVELOPING A STRATEGY

Once you have decided which funding sources will be included on your list, it is necessary to develop a plan of action, or strategy. Obviously, it is necessary to sort the due dates in order to address those that must be submitted first. However, a good strategy is more than that. It is a specific outline of what steps should be taken and in what order. In essence, it is a work plan for requesting funds from all of the sources that made the cut in the evaluation process as discussed previously. The following rules should be followed in developing and carrying out your strategy:

- Develop a two-page letter of inquiry that needs to be modified only slightly for most of the private foundations on the list.
- Plan to send the letter of inquiry to all of those private foundations for which that is the first method of contact and for which no specific due date is given.
- Set up a calendar that shows the due dates for letters of inquiry to those foundations with deadlines for the receipt of those letters and send them as they come due.
- Plan to personally contact those foundations that require proposals rather than letters of inquiry in order to determine your chances of getting funding. Once these conversations have been held, decide whether it is worth committing your resources to an application.
- Determine which governmental sources represent the best chance of funding. For those that accept applications on a continuous basis,

begin with the best fit and work your way down. For those applications that have specific due dates, plan to have the resources committed at that time so that those submissions can be made.

- For those sources that are open for applications only once a year, plan to keep checking every two weeks or so to see if the solicitation announcement has been made. Quite often, these yearly submissions are not tied to an exact date. Some try to invite applications at approximately the same time every year. More often, however, administrative and fiscal matters can cause the solicitation to be made earlier or, more commonly, later, than twelve months after the last solicitation. Some of these programs can actually skip a year or it may be as much as eighteen months between solicitations. I have even seen grant solicitations withdrawn after being published.

- If you find yourself in the position of having a number of sources with applications coming due at the same time, figure out a way to commit staff resources so that all applications can be submitted. Make the decision that the job will be done and that you will find a way to do it. You will regret it if you let a good chance slip away. The application that you decide you do not have time to do may very well be the one that would have provided the funding. Remember, this is just for a short period, and you will get through it. If you really feel that you could not do this yourself, try to farm it out to other staff or consultants.

I will illustrate these principles through the means of an example that happened to me recently. A very dedicated client of mine is working to find the funds for a residential facility for veterans with challenges such as homelessness, joblessness, addictions, and emotional disorders. Before he engaged my services, the city government was kind enough to undertake a grant search for him. My job was to develop a strategy based on the sources that were identified.

The search identified the following as potential governmental sources of funds: two programs of the Department of Housing and Urban Development, two programs of the Department of Labor, one program of the U.S. Veterans Administration, one program of the National Institutes of Health, and two programs through the state of Maryland. In addition, it was suggested that Blue Cross and Blue Shield as well as the Robert Wood Johnson Foundation would possibly fund the project. The list also included a number of other more local sources. These included other private foundations, fundraisers, veterans' service organizations (such as the American Legion and the Veterans of Foreign Wars), fraternal organizations, veteran-owned businesses, churches and other faith-based organizations, the United Way, and public financial support.

The interesting thing was that a number of the federal programs did not have current open solicitations. In each case, the time period for the current year's application cycle had passed, with no indication of when the next funding round would be. I went back through the entire list and verified that the project was eligible for assistance under each program. I then looked to see if a local match was required, what types of activities could be undertaken, and any special conditions that would have to be met.

The following is a brief excerpt from my letter detailing a suggested strategy:

Recommendations

I would recommend that you authorize me to undertake the following:

- An expanded foundation search that will include foundations that give on a national basis
- Preparation of letters of inquiry to both the Bateman and Winston Foundations
- Continuous monitoring of the following programs in order to determine when the next application cycle will be: HUD Supportive Housing Program; DOL Homeless Veteran Reintegration Program; DOL Veterans Workforce Investment Program; Homeless Veterans Grant Per Diem Program; the Robert Wood Johnson Foundation; and the Maryland HOME Program
- Ascertain whether your agency can be on the list of facilities receiving funding under the Maryland Emergency and Transitional Housing Program
- begin planning for a February application to the Community Foundation of the Eastern Shore

You and I would need to discuss whether my assistance is required for the NIH Substance Abuse grant. We should also discuss whether you would like to submit an application under CDA's Shelter and Transitional Housing Facilities Grant Program. This application is complex and for your project would only fund rehabilitation and capital equipment costs. I feel that this application could not be submitted until you have site control.

In order for the reader to better understand these recommendations, I would like to note that the Bateman and Winston foundations are located in the home state (Maryland) of the client. The search material that I was given only included the Robert Wood Johnson Foundation and no other private foundations. However I also did my own search on foundations within the state, and was frankly surprised to find only two sources. I expected to find many more, and thus not need to search for foundations that give this type of assistance on a national basis.

BEING REALISTIC ABOUT YOUR CAPACITY TO CARRY OUT A FUNDING STRATEGY

Once the strategy has been developed, it is necessary to analyze how your resources match up with the work you will have to do. In the sections above, I advocated doing everything possible to commit resources in order to not miss out on any available funding. In this section, I will be more specific about how you can determine your ability to take on the ambitious project of applying to multiple grant sources. Obviously, if your analysis shows that your organization is unable to carry out the strategy fully, it would be foolhardy to try to do so. You will need to look at the manpower, skills, capabilities, and experience contained within your organization. In addition, your budget needs to be large enough to give you the proper equipment and supplies with which to work. If lack of funds does not allow you to purchase modern technology that will make your job easier, it is more productive to think about how to improve that situation first. Building organizational capacity takes time. Throw away your preconceived ideas and see the big picture.

The advantages of making a structured analysis of capability are as follows:

- Being prudent about committing resources will allow the organization time to develop capacity naturally and without pressure.
- The funding will probably be approved eventually anyway.
- The organization will avoid any missteps that will give funding agencies a poor impression.
- The organization will be able to focus on "first things first" and build its strengths in order to prepare for a productive fundraising effort.

If an organization tries to take on a major grant seeking effort before it is ready, the following chain of unfortunate circumstances is likely to occur:

- Staff will feel overwhelmed and therefore perform poorly.
- This will lead to a lack of credibility with the funding agencies.
- This will in turn impact your ability to get future grants.
- All of these unfortunate events will cause poor morale among the team.
- None of this has gotten the problem solved.

This can be summed up in one sentence—be ambitious and work hard, and do things in logical steps as you are able.

MAKING THE BEST USE OF RESOURCES

It stands to reason that the grant writer will need to keep his resources in mind when developing the strategy. I am recommending that every source that looks promising should be approached with a letter of inquiry or an application as the case dictates. As the strategy unfolds, it is essential to keep in mind how staff capacity and other resources should be allocated to keep up with the demands of that strategy. As in anything else, good planning is absolutely essential.

Some factors to consider when deciding how to utilize personnel to best advantage are as follows:

- strengths and weaknesses of the team
- team experience
- team level of expertise
- team work ethic
- individuals' dependability in meeting deadlines (this is very important)

In addition, you will need to consider how to allocate outside sources of help such as volunteers, consultants, other agencies, and cooperating organizations. It is prudent to be very cautious about using volunteers in grant writing unless they have a proven track record. Ideally, these volunteers should have had a number of years of successful grant writing and administrative experience. In regard to the cooperating organizations, it is necessary to have clear guidelines for the part each agency will play so as to avoid competition when teamwork should be the order of the day. Again, the "no surprises" rule governs. There is no substitute for clearly set out roles for each organization and the staff within that organization.

This is not a human resources book. However, I will say that developing and implementing a successful strategy depends very much on making the best use of resources—that is, assigning the work to those team members who are best suited to carry it out. In most cases, a quick reading of the strategy will immediately produce some ideas as to which team members are best suited for which tasks. Ideally, the organization has a mix of skill levels and expertise in various areas that can be utilized to completely implement the strategy.

The list of positive attributes desired in your team cuts across all professions and is not unique to grant writing. However, the following specific skills are especially important ones for a grant writer to have:

- ability to communicate clearly in writing
- ability to locate research data
- commitment to meeting deadlines with no excuses
- skill in reading and understanding sometimes complicated and obscure regulations
- attention to detail

The organization will want to assign only the very best members of the team to implement the grant strategy. If some of the best staff have duties other than grant writing, try to temporarily assign their regular duties to someone else while the strategy is being carried out.

TAKING RISKS VS. BEING PRUDENT WITH RESOURCES

Like many other terms, "taking risks" as opposed to "being prudent" are subject to many different definitions and have relative meanings at best. As with everything else, it is best to strike a balance between the two. Examples of taking risks when applied to the grant field are as follows:

- reassigning a staff member to write a grant application for a highly competitive program when their other work, such as fundraising, is essential to the agency
- using needed capital to buy equipment in advance of a grant approval in order to show readiness, particularly when the grant program is very competitive
- committing to matching funds that your agency does not have readily available or cannot afford

Being prudent with resources generally entails being conservative and not taking chances on grant programs that are not likely to yield any funds. The only problem with this is that there are absolutely no sure things in the grant world, not even in formula programs. In those cases, funding may dry up, there may be a performance issue, or the application may not have been completed correctly. Taking chances is what we grant writers do. It is very rare to find any program that has enough funds to approve even 50 percent of the applications that come in. I have seen many cases where only 1 out of every 7, 9, or even 10 applications is approved. Therefore, the grant writer who is too prudent with resources will definitely miss out on a lot of funding.

The following rules have worked for me:

- For programs where a cash match is optional, if the agency is unable to provide the cash match, do not be afraid to say so. This will be taken into consideration during the review process and does not necessarily remove the application from consideration.

- Do not commit resources for a project in advance of receiving funding approval. Most grant programs will not allow reimbursement for expenses made before the execution of the grant agreement.
- If in doubt about whether there are sufficient resources for the project itself, it pays to submit the application anyway. You are not committed to accept the grant until you sign the grant agreement. The landscape may have changed significantly between the time of application submittal and approval.
- If you wish to receive grants, you will have to regularly submit applications to very competitive programs. There is no way around this.
- Investing in professional advice and taking grant writing courses will pay off handsomely.

In allocating resources for grant seeking, be aware of the interests of either the taxpayers (in the case of governmental applicants) or the board members and investors (in the case of private foundations).

Chapter Seven

Tools of the Trade

DEMOGRAPHICS AND OTHER RESEARCH

One of the most critical elements of any proposal is solid statistical documentation. This is the most compelling way to make the case as statistics are a common denominator that can be used to compare apples to apples and oranges to oranges. Most grant applications require some sort of numerical data. Solid documentation of this type is one of the most convincing ways for a grant writer to make a compelling argument for a project because it makes the need seem believable and more real.

An example of how this works would be the hypothetical case of a grant writer who is trying to show that the majority of residents of a particular neighborhood are of low- and moderate-income status. The proposal writer would need to gather statistics from a recognized source to document this. Data from the Census offers information on household and family income for various geographies from the block level up to the national level. This is the most widely recognized source of demographic, social, and economic data in the United States. In our hypothetical example, if the proposal writer is lucky, the neighborhood in question may conform to Census geography. It is possible that a particular block group may comprise the neighborhood in question. Where this is not the case, the writer may need to work with individual blocks in order to build data that corresponds to the neighborhood in question. A detailed discussion on what information is available through the Census and how to use it is provided later in this chapter.

The grant writer may also use other indicators of economic distress such as the level of poverty, the age of housing in the area, the median value of the houses, median contract rent, number and percent of housing units lacking complete plumbing or kitchen facilities, and number of families not owning a vehicle.

The writer of a grant proposal for a heritage tourism project, such as the development of a small local museum, could use this same information in order to make the case that the area in which it is located exhibits economic distress and therefore show the need for a tourist attraction. The application should document that promotion of heritage tourism will bring in needed dollars to stimulate the local economy. In this instance, because we are talking about an area broader than just a single neighborhood, it would be appropriate to use unemployment statistics, which are available by county from the Bureau of Labor Statistics (U.S. Department of Labor).

In addition, the grant writer would need to provide information documenting a projected increase in tourism as a result of the project being funded. In order to make an effective case, baseline data showing the number of visitors to the area prior to the inception of the project is essential. State and local tourism offices could assist in developing projections that would show the positive impact of the proposed project. In addition, local and state economic development departments can provide useful information regarding the number of new tourism-oriented businesses that are likely to open as a result. These projections, although very educated guesses in some instances, are necessary in order to make the case that the project is needed.

Applications for assistance with law enforcement projects will use documentation from departmental reports that show the level of various categories of crime in a community over a certain period of time. This data is generally collected by the department on a routine basis anyway. The police department may also cite studies from other areas around the country that document the positive results of projects similar to that being proposed.

Census Data

The Census data is the "gold standard" for statistical documentation. A wealth of information may be obtained from the Web site at http://www.census.gov. The Census Bureau, a subdivision of the U.S. Department of Commerce, collects a wide variety of information from U.S. residents every 10 years. This data is collected for almost every conceivable combination of variables and covers such items as total population, gender, race, housing conditions, income, personal transportation, commuting patterns, ethnicity, language and educational attainment. The Census information is very important in that it is used to allocate federal funds to smaller jurisdictions. It is beyond the scope of this chapter to discuss the vast multitude of variables that are available in Census data—this is just a brief summary of the main categories of information.

If the grant writer needs assistance in interpreting the data or finding a specific data set, it is possible to contact Census Bureau staff for help. However, many states have specialists, most of them in the planning departments, who are happy to assist local governments and nonprofits in finding appropriate documentation of the need for a particular project. I have found this avenue to be somewhat more helpful than going to the federal level. No doubt this is due to the sheer volume of requests the Census Bureau receives.

Census data is collected for several different types of geographies. The Census block is the smallest component of geography for which data is collected. These geographies continue up in size to the block group, Census tract, Census-designated place, Census incorporated place, consolidated city, Minor Civil Division, county or county equivalent, state, division, region, and the nation. In addition, data is given for what are referred to as American Indian Areas, Alaska Native Areas, Hawaiian Homelands, and Alaska Native Regional Corporations. Some data may be suppressed at the block level due to the laws protecting the privacy of individuals and families. Data normally given in larger Census geographies is not provided for blocks if these individuals can thereby be identified.

Counties and municipalities may find the two- to four-page fact sheets on their jurisdiction very useful. This is very basic data that gives the most needed demographic, social, economic, and housing information. Some of these fact sheets will also contain the same data for either the state in which the locality is located or for the United States as a whole. These comparisons are invaluable when the grant writer must make a case that the levels of distress in his or her community are higher than in the state or nation. Distress, like many other things, is relative. Just giving certain factors such as median household income and poverty level in isolation does nothing to show that the area in question is any needier than any other area. The grant writer must make the case that the level of distress is such that the application should be given a priority and eventually funded.

Information is given in the form of maps as well as tables in seemingly endless combinations. The basic Census information is given in four separate files referred to as, not surprisingly, Summary File (SF) 1, Summary File 2, Summary File 3, and Summary File 4. SF 1 and 2 contain what is referred to as 100 percent data, which means that all citizens are required to answer those questions. SF 3 and 4 are sample data, with only one household in six being required to answer the questions that are contained on what is referred to as the "long form."

As one can imagine, when we approach the time for the next Census, the current data is in actuality quite out of date. However, it is still used for grant purposes until the next Census information is available. This is necessary in order to achieve consistency. In order to help ensure greater accuracy, the Census Bureau provides interim projections and estimates. These "estimates" are defined as the Bureau's data that shows the current picture of a certain demographic. "Projections" on the other hand, are the Bureau's predictions for what a particular demographic will be at a certain time in the future.

The American Community Survey (ACS) is different from the population estimates referred to above. Those estimates are considered to be "official" and supersede the ACS if there should be a conflict. Only certain communities, generally larger jurisdictions, are surveyed for ACS. Certain types of data are published at one-year intervals, while other data is published at three-year and five-year intervals. The ACS contains many of the main demographics contained in the regular decennial Census such as population size, age, race, and gender. The Economic Development Administration of the U.S. Department of Commerce requests that grant applicants utilize ACS data if it is compiled for their community.

In addition, the Census Bureau publishes an economic Census every five years, with the last one having been disseminated in 2007. This material is very exhaustive and thorough and contains data by industry sectors. This information includes, for each sector, the number of employees, the number of establishments, size of the payroll, receipts, and a wealth of other information.

Bureau of Labor Statistics

The Bureau of Labor Statistics (BLS), a subcabinet agency of the U.S. Department of Labor, provides much valuable information regarding the nation's economy and workforce characteristics. This information can be accessed at http://www.bls.gov and is quite useful to grant writers working on economic development projects. For example, a municipality that is seeking grant and/ or loan funds to assist a prospective new business may find this data useful in persuading the company that economic conditions in a particular area are favorable to that industry.

BLS started compiling much of this data as far back as 1947. The numerous tables and data sets that are available from the Bureau of Labor Statistics are published at varying intervals. Some data, like the unemployment rate, is published once a month. Other information is published quarterly or annually.

The only disadvantage to this data is that many of the smaller levels of geography are not surveyed. Depending upon the data set, information is available down to the county, Metropolitan Statistical Area (MSA), or Metropolitan Division level. The Census Bureau defines a Metropolitan Statistical Area as a "core area containing a substantial population nucleus with adjacent communities having a high degree of economic and social integration." An MSA must contain at least one urbanized area with a population of at least 50,000.

The following is a partial listing of the data that can be obtained from the Bureau of Labor Statistics:

- Consumer and producer price indices (shows the average change in prices received by domestic producers for their output)
- The change in U.S. import and export price indices
- Consumer expenditure information (includes buying habits, expenditures, income and demographics of purchasers)
- Unemployment rate
- American Time Use Survey (includes time spent doing professional work at home and at the workplace, as well as time spent on household duties and child care)
- Employment statistics, including the number of employees in various sectors of the economy
- Payroll levels
- Job openings and labor turnover rates
- 10-year occupational employment projections
- Mass layoff survey
- Workforce injuries
- Productivity

Next to the Census Bureau, the BLS is the most comprehensive and helpful statistical research resource for grant writers. In addition to these reports, the Bureau of Labor Statistics publishes a number of reports dealing with the labor market. I would recommend that the grant writer sign up to receive the periodic updates available.

Other Research Resources

There are a number of other research resources at the state and local levels. Most states have a department dealing with planning issues, and these departments are generally the repository for Census information and other statistical data pertaining to that state. In addition, other Cabinet-level state agencies collect information dealing within the area that they regulate. I will give some illustrations in order to point the grant writer in the proper direction. For example, the state agency charged with regulating local water and wastewater plants would collect information on the following: description of each municipal or county plant along with its capacity, number of well and septic system permits issued (in the case of those areas not served by public water and sewer), number of water and wastewater treatment plants in violation of environmental regulations, and environmental information regarding bodies of water within its jurisdiction.

State law enforcement agencies compile information on the crime rate within the state, broken down by jurisdiction and classification of crime. The court system also maintains data on the number of cases heard, disposition, and the overall conviction rate.

State education agencies will maintain data on the schools in the state, the number of pupils, dropout rate, level of achievement accomplished, and statistics dealing with pupil transportation.

State and federal grantor agencies are also useful sources of data when it comes to case studies of projects that they have funded, though the willingness to share these case studies depends on the individual agency. This information helps the grant writer to learn from the mistakes of others and see what types of projects have been the most successful in alleviating a similar need in other areas of the country. Because you will be seeing those projects that have been successful in obtaining funding, you can be comfortable in using the design principles and methodology utilized by the administrators of those projects.

Another way to research other projects that can serve as a model is to look at professional trade journals in the relevant field. Nearly all of these publications feature articles regarding successful projects carried out by local governments and nonprofits. It might take the grant writer a while to find a project with direct applicability, however, a determined effort over time pays off.

Local governments are also a good source of research data, being able to offer either information reported to them by other entities or data collected to report to the federal and/or state governments. One excellent example of this is the publication "Brief Economic Facts," which is published for each county in the state of Maryland. This four-page document is developed jointly between the county government and the Maryland Department of Business and Employment Development. It contains a wealth of information in a standard, easy-to-use format.

Other examples of data generated by local governments are as follows: number of businesses licensed; crime statistics, which are reported to state agencies; the economic impact of tourism; and the number of housing code violations.

Some of the best data is that generated for a specific project that deals directly with the extent of the need. One example of this would be a "windshield survey," which, as its name implies, involves the surveyors driving through a particular neighborhood. These surveys are useful in determining the condition of housing as well as streets, sidewalks, and curbs.

For other projects, the need may be documented by taking an opinion survey. This would express the views of the residents of a certain area as to the need for certain services or infrastructure. Most agencies greatly value the views of the public that a project is designed to benefit. Letters of support, which in some cases are required and in other cases are optional, bring in the critical component of public opinion. This type of "on the ground" information is very convincing and will carry a great deal of weight with the funding agency.

Other programs, most notably the CDBG program, require income surveys for projects geared toward a specific neighborhood for which Census data cannot be used, is not relevant, or is not available.

Social service agencies can use their own data to justify new programs or the continuation of current programs. For example, the length of the waiting list for a housing voucher program can be the most convincing evidence of the need for additional housing vouchers. In addition, these agencies will track the characteristics of their clients that qualify them for the agency's programs and services. These characteristics may include income level, disabled status, employment status, or female head of household status.

DOCUMENTATION

This is nothing more and nothing less than proof or backup for what the grant writer says in an application and is invaluable in establishing credibility. This also pays off not just in the current application round but in subsequent rounds, as funding agencies begin to see that your agency always presents truthful and complete information.

Examples of documentation include the following:

- Proof of matching funds (this can be a letter from the funding agency or a grant agreement)
- Rejection letters from other funders
- Memorandum of Understanding with a cooperating agency that shows that the applicant has solid partners to carry out the project
- Resumes of key project personnel
- Engineer's or architect's estimate of costs
- Income survey results
- Census or Bureau of Labor Statistics maps and tables
- Other research results
- Letters of support from community organizations or groups that will benefit from the project
- Drawings or renderings of the facility to be constructed or rehabilitated with the grant
- Map(s) of the project area
- Progress reports for previous grants from the agency from whom the funds are being requested
- Photographs
- Organizational documents (charter, Articles of Incorporation, Bylaws)

- Certificate of Good Standing issued by the state (for nonprofits; this may have different names in different states)
- Environmental review documents
- Financial statements, audit reports, operating budgets and tax returns
- Proof of 501 (c) (3) status
- List of Board of Directors
- Resolution of support from a local government or the Board of Directors of a nonprofit organization

Not every grant application requires all of the above documentation. It is wise to gather attachments as one of the first steps in the application process. This is because these items may take some time to get as the grant writer often has to request them from other departments of the organization or other entities entirely, such as an accounting firm, engineer, or architect. This process can sometimes be nerve-wracking, as these other entities do not feel the same sense of urgency as does the grant writer with an imminent deadline. The grant writer should contact the appropriate office or agency as early as possible, impress on them the need to meet the deadline (the project will not be funded if this does not happen—who wants to have that responsibility on their shoulders?), and then follow up as frequently as necessary. Do not feel as if you are bothering your associates—you have a job to do. They have a job to do also—it is to help you win the grant dollars. Incomplete applications are not reviewed.

GRANTS.GOV

The online application submittal process on Grants.gov can be quite complex. At the present time, only a few federal agencies are *requiring* that applications be submitted through this process. However, applicants *may* do an online submittal for every grant opportunity shown on Grants.gov. As may be expected, the process is not a simple one. In order to submit, applicants must first obtain a DUNS (Data Universal Numbering System) number, become registered through the Central Contractor Registry (CCR), and then become registered through Grants.gov itself. Appendix D takes the grant writer through the entire process, step by step. Perseverance will be needed but greatly rewarded.

I believe that in time all applicants for federal assistance will be required to utilize this process. In the meantime, the federal government is taking small steps toward this goal. Applicants for the Scenic Byways program monies, administered through the U.S. Department of Transportation, have been required to submit only the cover page through Grants.gov. Presumably, this is to allow grant seekers to become registered and familiar with the process.

Grants.gov received over 300,000 online applications during calendar year 2009. One of the major reasons for this heavy volume was the large number of grant solicitations after the passage of The American Recovery and Reinvestment Act in mid-February of 2009.

The system provides some very convenient features. It is possible to sign up for an e-mail subscription that gives periodic information on changes and improvements made to the site. The grant applicant may download application packages and save and complete them offline and then cut and paste when ready to submit online. I have found that this capability has several advantages. It reduces performance anxiety and cuts down on the possibility of having a narrative lost while writing online.

There are numerous resources available to help applicants through the process including animated tutorials, Web casts, and user guides. In addition, applicants can easily track their application once it has been submitted. I have found this to be an invaluable resource as it is certainly an improvement on one's options for checking on paper submissions. The applicant is promptly notified by email of the application's progress from level to level during the course of the review. Another useful feature of this site is that the "submit" button does not become active until the application has been completely and correctly filled out. This prevents many mistakes that are made in haste and regretted at leisure. I have seen a number of other programs that permit the applicant to make an online submission without completing the application. To their credit, the administrators of Grants.gov fully appreciate the complexity confronting grant seekers on their site, and appear to be working to correct this situation.

Several examples will serve to illustrate the pros and cons of using Grants.gov. Many last-minute problems can be eliminated by remembering to follow the requirement that registration in the Central Contractor Registry be updated every year. I have personally seen two instances in which this could have kept an applicant from submitting a funding request. In one case, a municipality wished to apply for funding to purchase equipment for its parks and recreation department without realizing that its CCR profile had not been updated in the past year.

The reason that this became such a problem was because they could not find their password or TPIN (Trading Partner Identification Number) in order to access their account. The process is relatively easy once one can gain access. This in turn would not have been such a problem had they been able to get through to the Central Contractor Registry. Due to a huge increase in call volume because of the many grant opportunities suddenly becoming available under The American Recovery and Reinvestment Act, the system was in gridlock for four or five weeks. E-mails were not answered, and when the municipality attempted to call the helpline they got a recording that basically told them to call back without giving them the opportunity to remain on hold or to leave a message. Finally, at the 11th hour, the town received its password and was able to access the system. This was a close call that highlights the necessity to do three things—plan ahead, plan ahead, and plan ahead.

I was told of another city in the south that needed to complete a new registration in order to apply for funding for an economic development project. They were not aware of the requirement to register in CCR until just a few weeks before the application due date. The Grant Administrator thought he had completed the process and indeed had received a message on the final screen that indicated that the registration had been successful. He stopped at this point but had to scramble when the staff person who was actually writing the application found that she could not access the system and that certain other steps had to be taken.

I am aware of a nonprofit that also almost missed their chance to apply through Grants.gov due to their registration in the system not being complete. At almost the very last minute, the director of the nonprofit was frantically working to complete the portion of the registration that authorized the grant writer to access the system and thus submit the application. This was also a very close call, but the job got done.

All of these anecdotes point up the need to be well-organized and allow plenty of time. A good rule of thumb here is that this process will probably take longer than you think. In addition, all kinds of factors outside of your control come into play here. Don't be caught unaware. Keep following the process closely every step of the way.

Chapter Eight

General Writing Tips

Writing seems to be one of those difficult jobs for many people. I will not speculate on why this is other than to say perhaps that it is not emphasized enough in our educational system. Perhaps many people have an innate fear of expression, afraid that others will say negative things about their work. Be that as it may, this is a skill (or art form) that can most definitely be learned. Fortunately, classes in writing abound. I will say more about that later. However, to begin, I would like to amuse the reader with a brief description of how I write.

First of all, I learned to write on the job when I started working in the Salisbury, Maryland, Mayor's office in 1977. Prior to that time, I had not done any significant writing with the exception of papers in high school and college. I do not remember feeling intimidated about having to write my first grant application. I just looked upon the exercise as simply answering a series of questions. Mentally, I broke the application down into the relevant sections and only thought about one section at a time.

I still organize my thoughts in that fashion and in my opinion, this helps to alleviate the anxiety that is naturally associated with writing a request for funds or a book such as this one. Although it may seem intimidating to write a book, it was actually easier than I expected. The main reason for this is that I spent a significant amount of time in the beginning organizing the topics and the order in which they would be presented. Having this framework has proven invaluable. As I wrote this book, I have seen that this original organization of chapters and subparts has stood the test and best represents the universe of topics to thoroughly cover all aspects of the grant writing profession.

Before writing each chapter, I jotted down a few thoughts for each section and did any research that was necessary. I then began writing this book the same way I do everything else—by dictation. I have a software package on my computer that allows me to dictate into a microphone and have the words appear on the computer screen. This is a very quick and easy way to write. My strategy was to work on the book for an hour or two per day for at least four days of the week. It is amazing how quickly a book can take shape with this type of steady, consistent effort.

Many people are not comfortable with dictation. Perhaps they feel that typing is more in tune with their pace of thoughts. This gives them the opportunity to continually check and reread what they have written. On the other hand, I am more comfortable with a faster pace. I just talk into the microphone and then go back and see what changes I want to make. I began dictating about 15 years ago and have become hooked. For whatever reason, I do very little rewriting. I will certainly edit or rewrite a few words or sentences, but in general, I do not do multiple drafts of the same grant application. This system has worked very well for me.

One of the most important factors in writing is to set aside time that is dedicated 100 percent to getting those words on paper. I realize that, in some organizations, this may be extremely difficult to do. However, if your employer realizes how important your writing will be, given the fact that it will hopefully bring in substantial amounts of money, he or she will do whatever is necessary to create an atmosphere in which you can work in an uninterrupted fashion. Because I work at home, I now have this luxury. In my first job, I sat out in the reception area with the secretary. People were coming back and forth all the time to see the Mayor. Naturally, seeing me sitting in that area seemed to be an open invitation to sit down and talk. This made it extremely difficult for me, but I had no other choice. Somehow the work got done. Of course, I did not have to write every day. I did a number of administrative tasks as well.

I have found that many people have a problem with being easily distracted. This has not been helped by the availability of the new social networking sites. I have seen and heard of people making postings at the altar while getting married, during childbirth, and while teaching a class. A colleague told me a very funny story relating to a Twitter friend of hers who was writing a very long and complex federal grant application. It seemed that this friend was somewhat of a procrastinator. This application called for 45 pages of technical narrative. Naturally, this required a great deal of concentration. The application was due on October 15 of that year. However, it appeared that he had completed only 10 pages by October 1. He spent more time making postings about how much more work he had to do than he did in actually writing. He would talk about how he was going to closet himself and write for an entire weekend and then post frequently during that weekend about how many more pages he had to go. He made six postings in one day about this, saying "thirty-five pages to go to go," thirty-four pages to go," and so forth.

The message here is to not let distractions take you away from your writing. This is an exercise in which concentration is utterly essential. I realize that it is difficult, but one must be disciplined in order to succeed at writing. The writer has to be willing to push everything else aside.

It stands to reason that persons with the following traits will be the most successful at writing: ability to think critically, ability to communicate, giving attention to detail, patience, having a good vocabulary, being well-read, and being well-grounded in English.

Despite the fact that I learned successfully on the job, the single biggest predictor of success at writing is the completion of writing courses. It is also helpful to first take some English classes if you not feel as if your schooling has prepared you adequately for a career in writing grant applications. In fact, I would recommend that the aspiring grant writer take at least two English classes as well as a writing course if some catch-up work is required. However, if you have successfully written memoranda, letters, and brief reports in a previous job, it may not be necessary to take the English classes. Likewise, if you have taken the required number of college-level English classes, you most likely will not need to repeat them in order to embark on a writing career. I would still recommend a course in creative writing. If you are fortunate enough to live in a community that has a community college or university, those institutions would be your best bet.

BE SPECIFIC AND GIVE CONCRETE EXAMPLES

I will have more to say on the importance of being specific in the next chapter. However, this advice definitely has its place in a chapter on general writing principles as well. There is no better way to illustrate this than to give two examples of how to describe the same project—a mentoring program for victims of domestic violence. The first example is the "fuzzy" one:

> The Newland Shelter for Victims of Domestic Violence needs money for its programs. We help victims of domestic violence and their children. The shelter fills a big need in the community. Our clients are very grateful for the help that they receive from us.

This type of nondescriptive paragraph raises more questions than answers. The following items are missing from this description: amount of funding being applied for, exactly how the funds will be used, description of the full range of services given at the shelter, estimated number of potential clients, and the number of persons on the waiting list.

The following is a vastly improved project description:

The Newland Shelter for Victims of Domestic Violence is applying for $30,000 in order to hire a counselor who will work twenty-five hours per week to train our clients in job-seeking skills. The shelter provides housing and meals for a two-year period for victims of domestic violence and their children. While our clients are resident here, they must take classes in child care, financial management, housekeeping, and other life skills. In addition, we provide a comprehensive counseling program which helps them to overcome emotional problems associated with the abuse they have endured. This grant will enable the new counselor to train all fifty of our clients in job seeking skills. Due to limited funding, we are unable to serve the sixty-five persons on our waiting list.

It is patently obvious that the funding agencies will be much more likely to approve an application that contains the second example. It would be next to impossible to get funding based on the description given in the first paragraph. This, like so many things in this book, is just common sense. Grant makers want to know the exact picture and do not like vague writing.

THE IMPORTANCE OF PERFECT SPELLING, GRAMMAR, AND PUNCTUATION

This is another one of those commonsense axioms—namely, that any writing should have perfect spelling, grammar, and punctuation. However, I have seen a number of grant applications where the spelling, grammar, and punctuation leave something to be desired. This might range from just a couple of very obvious errors all the way up to a piece of writing that is filled with mistakes.

In order to be taken seriously as a writer, you must absolutely be sure that your writing contains no misspellings, no grammatical errors, and no punctuation mistakes. While the content of a written piece is definitely the most important part, it is hard to be taken seriously if these other aspects are poorly done. This gives the impression of someone who does not know how to write properly and who has not had the proper training to establish their credibility. A certain amount of effort is necessary to establish one's threshold credibility and skill at a local level. As one goes higher up the ladder, the amount of effort and skill required to succeed will increase. Even one typographical error or misspelling can make you look as if you are not professional. *There must be no errors in spelling, grammar, or punctuation.*

One of the best ways to learn how to write is to read a good book on grammar. This is a relatively easy and inexpensive way to get started. It is also very helpful for the writer to keep a thesaurus close at hand while working.

WRITING COLLABORATIVELY

In this section, I will discuss two types of collaboration. One involves a scenario where a grant writer needs assistance from others to put a proposal together. This may involve subject matter experts who will provide information for certain sections of the application. The other type of collaboration is where a committee, such as the Board of Directors of a particular organization, will either critique the work of the grant writer or actually write the proposal themselves. Before I discuss the advantages and disadvantages of each, I would like to say that writing collaboratively is fraught with pitfalls and must be handled carefully in order to avoid hurt feelings, miscommunication, and a poor product.

The first example is by far the easiest to manage. The grant writer will see that he or she needs help with a particular part of the application. Let us say input is needed from program officers of a nonprofit who may have run projects similar to that for which funding is currently being requested. Information regarding the successes and failures of those projects is very germane to the current grant application. In addition, other staff members of the same organization may be called upon to provide information regarding the evaluation plan. Those persons who will be administering the project may be asked to provide information on their background and training in order to establish their credibility.

In order to ensure success for this type of collaborative writing, it is necessary that one person—that is, the grant writer or grant administrator—be in charge of the process. She would request assistance when needed and then incorporate the information into the application. Ideally, those contributing would understand that they are merely being asked to provide information as opposed to writing the application. This should help to alleviate any ego issues. In most cases, contributors to the application are recognized for their expertise in a particular area. The grant writer should make it clear that their assistance is greatly appreciated and that it is recognized that they are taking time from their own jobs to help. Expressing a sense of gratitude will go a long way toward eliminating any problems.

In order to save everyone's time, it is often desirable to ask the subject matter experts to make their contribution in the form of a list of bulleted points. The grant writer can make their job even easier by volunteering to discuss the expert's contribution in person or over the telephone, take notes, and then actually write that section.

It depends upon the organization whether the grant writer's work is reviewed or edited by senior staff. In many cases, the signing authority is someone other than the grant writer (i.e., the Mayor, County Council President, or Chairman of the Board of Directors). This provides an additional level of review that can be quite helpful.

The other type of collaborative writing is considerably more complicated. It involves a committee. I am sure that the readers have heard the expression "writing by committee." I have very rarely encountered this type of mass confusion. The reason for this is that it is just too difficult for a group of people, however small, to actually write from scratch. I have seen cases where different persons on a committee are individually responsible for particular sections of a document. The group as a whole would then critique each section. The problem with this is that it is hard to mesh a series of sections written by different persons into a coherent document that sounds as if it was written by only one person.

For this very reason, it is much more productive to have the committee critique the work of one person. Most of the committees I have seen welcome this with open arms and are relieved to not have the responsibility of actually writing the document. Even so, this type of collaboration can be very tricky, complicated, and prone to disagreements among the members. In order to alleviate these concerns, it is more productive to have a small group with a designated leader. Ideally, the committee should be picked so as to not contain persons who have an "ax to grind" or who are in a situation that would interfere with their ability to be impartial.

I have seen a number of situations where a grant writer's work is critiqued by persons who are either not familiar with grant writing or with the particular program from which funds are being requested. I have actually seen situations where critiques are given without the reviewer feeling the need to consult the program guidelines or even the grant application questions. This is clearly not in the best interests of the applicant organization. I would strongly urge grant seekers to put ego aside and work in a positive collaborative environment that will best ensure the success of the grant application.

In the 1980s, I became familiar with the work of a nonprofit whose mission was to assist homeless people in locating transitional housing. It was necessary to write a grant application for funds for operating costs during the coming year. They had a volunteer grant writer who was thoroughly familiar with the program under which the application was to be submitted. This was a continuation grant that had been received for a number of years. The application was somewhat of a formality, as long as it was completed properly. It was thus not necessary to "re-invent the wheel" and undergo a great deal of stress and pain. The president of the Board of Directors of this particular organization was quite given to minute review of everyone else's work. Either she or someone she trusted would be tasked with critiquing every document that was sent out.

On the face of it, this sounds like she was being very prudent. However, she quite often took the advice of the layperson that critiqued the document rather than the expert who completed it. What ended up happening was that the experts hired by the group were minimized.

A board member who hoped to eventually become executive director was asked to review the application the volunteer grant writer had prepared. What ensued was almost comic. He made it clear that he was going to take a great deal of time to look over this application. Every few days the grant writer would receive by e-mail another section he had looked at. Each page would be full of revisions. He also suggested widespread changes in the order of the information presented. Although he had written a few grant applications, he was not at all familiar with the program to which the group was applying. As far as I know, he did not even have a set of the application questions in front of him when he made these critiques. In short, he was trying to turn what should have been a simple exercise into an agonizing process. Finally, the staff person who had secured the agreement for the funds found a tactful way to get the gentleman to back off. I am all for careful review and editing, sometimes from outside experts, however, valuable time is wasted when the reviewers are not qualified to review. I have seen so many instances where the process was made so much harder than it needed to be.

A friend in New England belonged to a performing arts organization that needed to prepare a rather lengthy federal grant application. The group hired a very well-known and reputable firm to handle the project. Needless to say, this firm charged substantial fees. Once the application was completed, the entire document was sent around to the entire board of approximately 15 people for review. Each of these people responded back with numerous comments and requests for revision. In some cases, the comments dealt with nuances of local color that the consultant could not have known. In a few instances, the consultant got her facts wrong. However, predictably, a number of comments showed the personal bias of the commenter.

The executive director, without evaluating the comments, incorporated them all into the final document. I remember wondering why he simply accepted all revisions. It was entirely possible that some comments would be objected to by the majority of the other members. Therefore, there was no opportunity for the board members to either accept or reject the comments made by the other members. Of course, to have done so would have been incredibly cumbersome. This example points out the fallacies of making the process too complicated. It should be just complicated enough to produce the best document possible.

My final example deals with a transportation committee composed of officials and private citizens from all over the county, including all of the municipalities. The purpose of this committee was to produce a transportation strategy for the county. However, there were some rumblings of dissent at even setting up this process due to the fact that individual municipalities felt that their sovereign right to administer their own government was being threatened. Indeed, at several stages of the project, concessions had to be made to the fact that certain things were mandated by law to be under the sole jurisdiction of the municipality in question. The reader can immediately see that this situation was fraught with possibilities for conflict. What ensued was a combative and sometimes almost vicious battle over the contents of the strategy. This document was also developed by a consultant and the members of the committee attacked the contents of the document when really they were concerned with preserving their autonomy. Extensive compromise and negotiation became necessary. It is always more difficult when parties reviewing or editing a document such as a grant application have other motives besides producing the best document possible. In an ideal situation, reviewers or editors should take an impartial attitude, and the writer should not take requests for changes personally, particularly if he has attained a certain level of skill in the profession.

EDITING

As in my comments regarding grammar, spelling, and punctuation, there is no substitute for being extremely careful and checking your work at least twice. I mentioned that I use a dictation software system on my computer. In the beginning, while it was getting used to my voice, it made a number of errors. With this system, it is recommended that all errors be corrected verbally so that the software will "learn from its mistakes." This is indeed what has happened. As time has gone on, its recognition of what I am saying has gotten extremely good.

However, it is still necessary to go through each document paragraph by paragraph in order to edit it. I review my work as carefully as possible the first time I go through it, but I learned a long time ago that the second edit is absolutely essential. For example, in a five-page document, I may find as many as five errors on the second review.

Because the grant writer wants to make as good an impression on the reviewer as possible, it is necessary to ensure that any writing is "letter perfect." As I have said before, small errors give the reader the impression that the writer is not attentive to detail and has sloppy work habits. This is why accurate editing is so important. It is worth taking the extra time to make that second review. These writing rules of thumb are obviously different for each individual writer. Like many other endeavors, we all develop our own individual style. What works for me may not work for you. In the final analysis, writing is a very individualized and personal process. Although there are some rules, many aspects of writing are not inherently "right" or "wrong."

RESOURCES FOR WRITERS

This section may arguably be the most important part of this chapter. In it, I will answer the question "I want to learn how to write. How can I do that?"

Of course, writing is partly science and partly art. Some aspects of it are extremely difficult to teach. One of the best ways to learn is by taking a class that will give plenty of hands-on instruction and allow ample opportunity to practice writing. It should be noted that the resources given in this section are by no means exhaustive. There are myriad online and print resources for both aspiring and experienced writers.

Writers' associations can be of immense benefit by providing moral support, information sharing, and referrals to other sources of information. There are several writers' associations that are national in scope and encompass all types of writing specialties. These are as follows:

- National Writers Association (http://www.nationalwriters.com)
- Association for Women Writers (http://www.naww.org)
- Association of Writers and Writing Programs (http://www.awp writer.org)

A number of other national writers' associations only focus on certain types of writing. A quick Internet search will show that there are associations that serve writers who cover the following topics: golf; boxing; football; education; gardening; medicine; outdoor topics; construction; public safety; food, wine, and travel; science; and Internet entertainment. There is even a special association for people who write about cats! In addition, there are local, state, and regional associations within some of these topics.

There are also local, state, and regional writers' associations that serve all types of writers. The best way to find this type of group is to conduct an Internet search or consult your local library.

If the aspiring writer does not wish to take a class at a local college or writing school, there are a number of online courses in technical writing. It is beyond the scope of this book to list the various courses available. However, I would strongly urge the prospective student to check out each possibility very carefully in order to ensure that the organization sponsoring the course is reputable and that past students are satisfied. It is also very important to check to see which are the most comprehensive, thorough, and in-depth. The qualifications of the authors of these courses should also be carefully researched. It is well worth taking the extra time in order to ensure that you are getting the best value for your dollar.

The following are additional online resources for writers:

- Grammar Now! (http://www.grammarnow.com)—writers can look up any word and see its usage and definition in many online dictionaries
- Guide to Grammar and Style (http://andromeda.rutgers.edu/~jlynch/writing)—a resource on the rules governing writing and grammar.

- http://www.forwriters.com—lists groups, markets, workshops, and writers' forums
- http://www.writing-world.com—shows resources available to help writers learn how to write and become published
- http://www.writing.com—an online community of writers
- http://www.writersdigest.com—contains news about conferences, blogs, community information, and tips on how to write better and get published. The Writer's Digest is also available as a magazine.
- http://thesaurus.com—an online thesaurus

Chapter Nine

Basic Elements of a Proposal

GENERAL GUIDELINES

Never underestimate the importance of doing a superlative writing job on the grant application. This is one of the most critical predictors of success. However, many people are under the impression that the grant writer's skill in writing is the only important thing. In my opinion, the most critical factor is a well-designed project that meets the identified need with the most economical use of resources. The best written proposal cannot disguise the fact that a project is ill-conceived and designed and will not accomplish the desired outcomes.

Poorly written proposals do sometimes get funded, despite popular belief. I have seen this happen several times. This is generally the case when the project itself is of such importance that the funding agency and the nonprofit or political jurisdiction basically agree prior to application submittal that the project must move forward. An application must still be written and submitted and must meet threshold requirements. Grant writers with the highest professional standards will still wish to do their best for this type of application. I have seen several examples of such applications that were clearly not the best effort of the grant writer, however. Regardless of the quality of the application, overriding public concern dictates that the funds must be set aside for these very important projects.

I am aware of a state program that is run basically in this fashion. The director stays in close contact with local officials around the state and works with them to identify worthy projects that will advance the goals of the program. He then asks for an application for these hand-picked projects. Once the application has been submitted, funding is all but assured unless an untoward event occurs. This official strives to fund projects that are located throughout the state so that no one geographic area is favored. His grant making is monitored by other state officials for compliance with the applicable regulations.

Another local official with whom I am acquainted has made an art out of receiving approval in principle from the funding agency prior to actually submitting an application. His contacts are so good that he regularly deals with cabinet secretaries and department heads at the state level on a daily basis. He is a "mover and shaker" within his state. However, he still insists upon quality grant applications.

Another example of a less than stellar application being funded would be a poorly written submission that is accompanied by a substantial amount of well-done supporting information. This supporting information could be an engineering study, a feasibility study, or an annual report that clearly shows the extent of the need. The point I am making here is that the skill of the grant writer is just one of several factors in whether a particular application will be approved. It is wise to keep this in mind so as not to become too invested in the results of one's application submittals.

This is not to say that one should not put 110 percent into the applications. It is okay to feel ecstatic when our applications get funded. We are only human. Our self-esteem is very important. However, it is necessary to keep the results of our grant seeking in perspective. Many, if not most, of the worthy projects I have seen in my career eventually get funded if the grant seeker is knowledgeable, experienced, versatile, and well connected with funding agencies.

The following steps should always be followed *before* beginning to write the proposal:

- Read the entire solicitation at least twice from beginning to end.
- Call or e-mail the contact listed in the solicitation in order to discuss the project and to make certain that it meets threshold requirements.
- Determine whether it is possible to gather the data and write the application by the deadline—the grant writer will need to consider his or her own schedule and pace of working as well as the availability of colleagues who will be involved in preparing the grant application.
- Determine the feasibility of obtaining statistical data to directly support the project.
- Determine the feasibility of obtaining supporting information from others.

All grant writers will eventually develop a working style that is comfortable for them. For me, I have found that things generally work better if

I begin a proposal by first requesting information from others, thus getting that process started in the earliest stages. I then begin to write the proposal and check in often with the others who must supply documentation. This documentation may include pictures, income surveys, studies, public hearing notices, annual reports, cost estimates, proof of matching funds, and letters of support. Unfortunately, I have found that others will generally wait until the last minute to submit their supporting information. This appears to be human nature. Fortunately though, I am hard pressed to think of too many instances where other professionals failed to come through with their piece of information.

One notable example of problems caused by other professionals concerns an accounting firm that was working with a county on a grant proposal to fund the development of a new park. The application required the preparation of an audit report, which was the responsibility of the accounting firm. Nearly every accountant that I have worked with is very responsive and works very hard to complete the financial information for a project on time. The grant writer was given approximately three weeks to complete the application. She called the staff accountant at the firm, expecting a return call within a day or so.

Much to her surprise, the days went by with no communication from him despite a second call made a few days after the first. He finally returned her call after about 10 days. By then, much valuable time had been lost. The grant writer obtained the necessary information from the accountant and incorporated it into the application. Keep in mind that he was well aware of the deadline. A couple of days prior to the due date, it came to the grant writer's attention that there was a problem with some of the information that the accounting firm had sent and that some revisions would have to be made. The accountant ended up sending the revisions three days after the due date! The county was forced to negotiate an amended submission with the funding agency. Fortunately, this option was open to them. The funding agency could have thrown the application out altogether. It is hard to imagine what people are thinking sometimes.

It has been my experience that most funding agencies, particularly governmental ones, are willing to give a bit of leeway when *minor* items do not make it into the application but are needed nonetheless. Notice that I am stressing the word "minor". I would certainly not encourage anyone to leave out anything significant and trust that the funding agency will accept it. My success has in part come from taking funding agencies and foundations at their word literally down to the last detail. However, I have seen instances where a client has sent the incorrect number of copies despite my instructions, and the funding agency has very graciously accepted the submission anyway.

It seems to be human nature to wait until the last minute to meet a deadline. Often times, the press of daily business, along with other deadlines that come prior to the one in question, sometimes make it difficult to give our-selves as much time as we would like. However, I would strongly urge all grant writers to at least make their request to others for supporting informa-tion as soon as possible, if not immediately after deciding to apply for a par-ticular grant. It takes discipline, but it is extremely helpful to set aside even a small amount of time each day to work on the grant application.

Allow me to tell an incident from my own career, which has only become funny after the passage of 25 years. It certainly was not funny at the time. As described previously in this book, I worked for a municipality and then a nonprofit prior to starting my own business. This nonprofit always applied for funds under yearly solicitation of the U.S. Department of Housing and Urban Development. In many cases my boss, who served as the Executive Director, and the Board of Directors did not actually make the decision on which project to apply for until a week or two prior to the deadline. I would always make several attempts to get a decision that would allow me adequate time to prepare a wonderful application.

These attempts were all doomed to failure. In fact, the Executive Direc-tor acted relatively unconcerned until they actually made the decision with a short time to spare. Just as if it were yesterday, I recall my boss saying calmly in the early stages of the process, "It's not time to panic yet." However, when the decision was made, she would come running into the office out of breath and say in a very loud voice "It's time to panic!" Oh, how I hated to hear those words! I especially dreaded the day before the application was due to go out. On those days, all would be pandemonium as we attempted to make the appropriate number of copies and get to the post office on time. This was due in part to the short lead time, but also to last-minute changes. I would strongly urge grant seekers to refrain from making last-minute changes just for the sake of making changes. It is hard to overestimate the value of think-ing things through early in the process.

However, there are those times when a last-minute rush is unavoidable. Grant writers should do their best to ensure that those times are rare. I viv-idly recall when a much respected client called me at 11:00 a.m. to let me know that the state was requesting a renewal application for a current grant. The only catch was that this was due by 3:00 p.m. The state was willing to receive the application by e-mail. Luckily, this was a very brief application comprised of only a cover sheet, a budget sheet and a four-page narrative. It also helped that I had worked on the original project and had had this cli-ent for a number of years, so I was familiar with their needs and problems. Needless to say, we made the deadline.

It is also important, when planning an application, to not let doubts creep into your mind as to whether you are up to the task. Of course you are. As long as a thoughtful assessment of the requirements of a particular grant ap-plication has been made, and you feel comfortable, just assume that it will happen. I have written more than 900 applications in the course of my career, and all of them have been submitted on time. It is important to not let fear and worry creep in. The grant writing field is particularly susceptible to these two feelings due to the constant pressure of grant deadlines.

I am sure that the reader would like some sort of estimate of the time involved in putting together the typical grant application. This is very tricky, as the length and complexity of applications can vary widely, not to mention the differences in working style and speed among individuals. Let us assume that you are able to set all other tasks aside (this is not often the case). A relatively straightforward application to a private foundation generally consists of a cover sheet, budget, budget narrative, five-page descriptive narrative, and attachments, which can include support letters, statistical data, financial statements, and organizational documents for the applicant. I would advise the grant writer to set aside an uninterrupted period of three work days to complete an application of this type. A more complex federal application, which can consist of as many as 20 to 25 pages of narrative, can consume two to three weeks.

Before we get into the specific portions of the grant application, it will be useful to briefly discuss methods for actual physical submission of the application. This should be thought out well in advance. Although this sounds like a very obvious statement, grant deadlines are, in nearly every case, nonnegotiable. Do not plan on receiving an extension. Be very aware that it is incumbent upon the applicant to ensure that the application reaches the funding agency on time. Applications that are submitted only online present fewer complications in this regard. However, it is very important to remember that extra time should be allowed in case of technical difficulties resulting from the malfunctioning of the online grant utility or an overload on the system due to the number of persons accessing it.

Most funding agencies will not accept faxed applications, due to the need to receive a submission with original signatures. When dealing with postal mail, it is wise to err on the side of caution. Although the vast majority of "snail mail" gets to its destination in the United States within a few days, I have seen enough exceptions to this to urge grant seekers to use overnight mail if they are within two or three days of the submission deadline. Do not let the postal workers reassure you that the package will get to its destination on time anyway. The consequences of an application arriving late and being disqualified are just too great to take the chance. It is well worth the relatively reasonable fee for overnight service in order to have no worries about timeliness.

If the grant seeker has been fortunate enough to have the application ready to go a week in advance, and it is being sent to within a few hours' drive, I would be comfortable sending it by regular mail. However, I would either request that someone at the funding agency sign a receipt or I would call my contact at the agency. Sometimes things can go awry between the mail room and the office to which the application is to be sent. Some programs request that an application be received by a certain day and time, and others request that the application be postmarked by a certain time. In the latter case, the grant seeker has only to ensure that the package is properly postmarked by the postal worker.

In most cases, it is a waste of time to physically take an application to the funding agency, unless it is due on that very day. I know some persons who are only comfortable if they hand deliver the applications. I have only done this three or four times in my entire career, usually because I happened to be passing through the city in which the funding agency was located on or around the due date.

I have only had one mishap with the mail. One particular application reached the federal funding agency in Washington, D.C., on time. I received the return receipt signed by someone in the mailroom. Of course, these signatures are usually illegible, and it is hard to track down the person who signed. In any case, this application did not make it from the mailroom to the reviewing office on time. The agency refused to consider the application for this reason. Most people would consider this to be most unfair. The application was not received on time due to problems within the funding agency and was not related to anything I or my client did.

I would like to make a few comments on writing style. It is very important to write in a style that conveys the urgency of the need and the necessity for the project. The application should be written with feeling and give a sense of the serious consequences to the beneficiaries if the project should not be funded. This is the "human side" of the request. It is very difficult, if not impossible, to teach someone to write with feeling. That generally comes about with practice and a passion for one's work. Some of the individual stories of the potential beneficiaries can be used to show the very serious and personal nature of their distress.

In order to maintain clarity, it is necessary to refrain from using jargon. For example, if you are writing an application on behalf of a law enforcement agency, do not use terminology that only law enforcement workers can understand. The application needs to be written so that the reviewers can understand it. It is also necessary to explain any acronyms. Do not assume that everyone knows the meaning of an acronym common to your profession.

It is very important to keep repeating throughout the application some of the wording used in the grant solicitation. For example, if the solicitation states that the funding agency wants to promote sustainable agriculture, the grant writer should use that term liberally throughout the application. In the same vein, suppose the solicitation also mentions that priority will be given to projects whose technology is transferable to other geographic areas. If this is the case, the grant writer should state that using the exact language contained in the solicitation. This will produce a feeling in the reviewers' minds that the project is exactly what they are looking for.

I would like to offer a final piece of general advice prior to going on to the discussion of specific parts of the application. The Golden Rule of grant writing is to *be specific*. Vague and general statements will not get the grant money. If the grant writer is working to make a specific point, he or she should be very clear, use statistical support and examples, provide a clear picture of the need, the project, and the outcomes.

I once saw an application completed by a novice grant writer. Although it was a relatively simple funding application, I found a consistent pattern throughout of avoiding answering the questions specifically. That application told a reviewer very little. For example, one section asked the applicant to provide information regarding its partners, presumably to at least get the names of these partners and their association with the organization. The grant writer wrote one sentence, "We have many partners." This is a very obvious failure to provide the level of detail that will enable a reviewer to get a clear picture of an organization and its proposed project.

Finally, I would like to point out the obvious—follow the formatting requirements and page limitations, and submit the number of copies being requested. Specific formatting requirements may include the font, font size, double spacing vs. single spacing, margins, page numbering, and headings. When the agencies request a specific format, they mean it. Follow the requirements. It would be a shame to waste all of that work to have the application thrown out on a technicality. There is often a page limitation for the entire application, or a limit for each section. It is *very* important to adhere to these page limitations because the application could be tossed out if these requirements are not followed.

LETTERS OF INQUIRY TO FOUNDATIONS

Most foundations require a letter of inquiry as the first contact. If the project seems to be within their guidelines and funding priorities, they will then invite the submission of a full proposal. In this section, I will give some basic pointers on how to write a compelling letter of inquiry.

First of all, the grant writer should restrict the length of this letter to no more than two pages if the guidelines do not specify. Some foundations will state in their guidelines that the letter of inquiry should be no more than one or two pages. In this letter, your only job is to convince the foundation that your project is a good fit with their fields of interest. In order to make the best impression possible, it is imperative to direct this letter to the proper person. Most good foundation search resources will list a contact to which correspondence should be addressed.

Prior to beginning the letter, a decision should be made on the amount to be requested. This will be dependent in large part on the resources of the foundation. Search material should discuss the total assets of the foundation, along with the average grant amount, the smallest grant, and the largest grant. If your project will cost $50,000, and you know that a particular foundation only has assets of $100,000 and an average grant amount of $10,000, that is the figure you should request. For larger foundations, it is okay to request the full amount of $50,000. Foundations like to know that a project will actually happen if funding should be provided. Therefore, if you are requesting funding from multiple sources, it is necessary to make this clear in the letter of inquiry. Likewise, if you have already secured part of the funding, it is important to state this. Provide as much detail as possible regarding the status of the other funding requests.

Try to be as descriptive as possible and make your project sound irresistible to the foundation. However, I have found that overly flowery language is somewhat insulting to the reviewer. It makes it appear that you are trying to cover up the fact that your project does not have much substance and that you are building a smokescreen to hide that fact.

The first paragraph should clearly state the purpose of the project so that the reviewer will know exactly what will be done. This is also the place for the total project cost and the amount requested from the foundation. Lastly, a couple of sentences regarding how the project fits with the foundation's funding priorities should be included. These basic facts are important to have in the very beginning, so that they will catch the reviewer's eye and she will want to read on.

The next paragraph should go into detail regarding the need for the project and include as much statistical information as possible. This is also the place to make a strong appeal to the emotions of the reader. It is wise to give one or two specific examples of the distress suffered as a result of the need for the project. This is where the "human factor" comes in. The grant writer will be wise to combine hard data and emotion in this section.

Following this, a history of your organization should be given. This should include a description of similar projects that have been successfully undertaken. This is also the place to discuss your organization's mission and its priorities. You want to convince the reader that your organization has the capacity to undertake the project, that your staff has the appropriate skill sets for the work, and that you will give it the priority it deserves so that it may be completed in a timely manner.

The next section of the inquiry letter should go into some detail regarding how the project will be implemented. It is important to detail each step in the process from beginning to end. By doing so, the reader may see the feasibility of the project and feel confident that your organization knows exactly what it takes to get the project completed on schedule and within the budget. Goals, objectives, and positive outcomes will also be discussed here.

Sustainability and evaluation should be discussed next. Having solid plans in place for both issues assures the foundation that your organization has thoroughly thought through the entire process. The foundation will want to know that resources have been identified to continue the project beyond the grant period and that a thorough evaluation will be performed in order to determine its effectiveness.

Close the letter by offering to meet with the foundation officials at their office, host a site visit, or discuss the project over the telephone. Emphasize your willingness to provide any additional information requested by the foundation.

The following sections pertain to the requirements for a full proposal to either a government agency or foundation. These are the most requested items, although specific questions may vary.

COVER LETTER

A cover letter is not required for every application. In some instances, the guidelines call for one. However, I generally do not send a cover letter with applications that have a cover sheet. The main purpose of a cover letter is to further confirm the fact that the application was indeed sent. Another benefit to doing a cover letter is to have an additional space in which to point out the merits of the project, as obviously the cover letter does not count in any page limitations.

One circumstance in which it is absolutely imperative to do a cover letter is when the applicant is sending copies of the application to the State Single Point of Contact, also sometimes referred to as the clearinghouse, or any other governmental entity that is required to review the application along with the funding agency. The purpose of the designated agency is to send copies of the application to various other state agencies to determine whether the proposed project is in conflict with any plans or policies of these agencies. The applicant should keep a copy of its letter to the clearinghouse in its files to document that this step was indeed taken. The funding agency to which the application is being submitted will often require a copy of the letter to the clearinghouse as well.

Not every state requires that this step be taken. Only federal applications are subject to this review. This law does not cover applications made to state programs. It is not necessary to take time to summarize the application within this cover letter. It is sufficient to merely make the statement that the clearinghouse is being sent the appropriate number of copies of the application and to mention the federal agency to which the application is being submitted.

Some states also require that the agency charged with overseeing historical preservation efforts be given the opportunity to comment. Again, copies of this letter should be saved for the applicant's files as well as submitted with the application in order to document the fact that that it was sent. A few brief sentences stating that the application is being submitted for review is sufficient.

COVER SHEET

Most governmental and foundation grants require some sort of cover sheet that requests basic information regarding the project and the applicant. In the case of federal applications, this is the Standard Form 424, which is included as part of Appendix C. Most cover sheets request at least the following information:

- contact information for the applicant
- contact information for the project director
- Employer Identification Number of the applicant
- amount requested
- title of the project and a brief description of no more than a few sentences

ABSTRACT

This is a brief summary of the application, generally running no more than two pages in length, although many solicitations limit the abstract to one page. This element of the application is not always required, and should only be prepared when explicitly requested in the grant guidance documents. In some cases, the specific points to be covered in the abstract are delineated by the funding agency.

When specific guidance is not given, the following items of information should be included:

- The heading should clearly state the title of the project, the funding agency to which the application is being submitted, the name of the funding program, and the name of the applicant.
- The first paragraph should be a summary of the activities to be undertaken with the funds as well as the amount applied for—it is helpful to funding agencies to know exactly where their money is going at the very beginning of the application. This provides clarity, which makes a positive impression.
- The second paragraph should briefly describe the need for the project and give statistical information to back this up.

- The third paragraph should delineate specific positive outcomes resulting from the grant.
- The fourth paragraph should briefly describe the capabilities and experience of the applicant organization, as well as the reasons why the applicant cannot afford to undertake this project on its own.
- The final paragraph should be a brief "wrap-up" that states how the project will be evaluated and then sustained after the grant period has expired.

After reading this chapter, it will become obvious that the abstract is no more than a very brief summary of each section of the application in turn. This is a very important part of any submission because it provides a brief, "at a glance" description that should make a positive impression in the very beginning.

STATEMENT OF NEED

Although this is one of the most important parts of any grant application, it also tends to be one of the most poorly written. One of the reasons for this may be that many grant writers just assume that the need for the project is obvious. Do not assume anything. The grant writer must make the case for both the need for the project and the need for financial assistance to do the project in a very clear, comprehensive, concise, and compelling manner. These are the four C's for writing any grant application. This section is no place for vague, general, weak, or "stretching" statements.

Grant reviewers are not fond of flowery language. They tend to regard this type of verbiage with suspicion. It is as if the grant writer does not really have anything substantial to say and relies upon words designed to disguise the fact that there is no substance to the proposal. Whenever I read something like that, I feel rather insulted, as if I had been confronted with a particularly bad sales pitch. What counts with grant reviewers is a simple, direct statement of the facts. Please let your facts shine through and speak for themselves. They do not need to be embellished or exaggerated. Do not, under any circumstances, tell falsehoods in your application. This will damage your credibility with the funding agencies and word will get around. Your success rate will plummet rapidly. At the risk of sounding redundant, I will say it again: it is not worth the risk.

As I have said before and will certainly say again, it is very important to be *specific*. The use of statistics, when available, makes a very compelling case. Individual histories and anecdotes are also helpful. In short, anything that can help the reviewer to get a clear picture of the project should be added to this section of the narrative. The basic elements of a well-written project-need section are just commonsense. They are as follows: general description of the situation, the number and type of people affected, the extent to which these people are affected, and what will happen if the project is not done.

I will now give some types of information that should be added to the needs statement for various special types of applications. For a project with a social services component, key information to be included in this section is as follows: number of persons on the waiting list for the specific services for which funding is requested; the income level or housing conditions of prospective beneficiaries; and the unemployment rate, median income, educational level and poverty rate for the area or group affected by the project.

Law enforcement applications will need to include information regarding the crime rate in the needs statement. Any type of trend in this crime rate should be discussed specifically, with numbers taken from actual reports to show the numerical and percentage increase or decrease in crime. Information should also be given on the impact of crime on victims. It would be helpful to include anecdotes that bring home the devastating impact that crime can have. These applications will be enhanced by also including information on the conviction rate as well as a measurement of damage inflicted by crimes in terms of lives lost, injuries, and property damage.

For historic preservation projects, it is essential to describe to what extent the targeted resource is threatened as well as its significance and the history that will be lost to posterity if it is not preserved. Heritage tourism projects involving, for example, a museum, will need to discuss the gap in educational interpretation the museum will fill, as well as its impact on the economy and its uniqueness to the area. For example, if there are no other facilities providing this exact type of interpretation within a hundred miles or so, that is significant and provides support for the need for the project.

Projects proposing economic development activities should provide new jobs or retain existing jobs. This should be well documented in the needs section by giving specific numbers and names of employers or potential employers. The existing unemployment rate and any trends in that rate in the past several months should also be discussed. Depending on the type of project, the grant writer may also wish to mention the quality of the work force in the area and the extent of training received by those workers.

The information described above will demonstrate why the project should be done. It is also extremely important to discuss the need for financial assistance in order to carry it out. The applicant must clearly demonstrate that without grant funding, the project will not move forward. If the applicant has been turned down by other potential sources, it is necessary to specify that and to include copies of the letters rejecting the request for funds. It is always helpful for agencies to know that they are not the only source that is being requested to provide funding. An applicant will have more credibility if it can be demonstrated that potential funding sources were carefully researched and a funding strategy was well thought out.

Another angle to demonstrate financial need is to show the allocation of funds in an organization's total budget in order to demonstrate that no applicant monies are available. This information will show that all available funds are going toward operating costs and cannot be used for new projects or that other needed projects are consuming the entire budget of the organization. In many cases, a copy of the applicant's most recent audited financial statement must be submitted along with the application.

In the case of municipalities or counties, information regarding the economic situation of the community is critical. If an area is considered to be economically disadvantaged and demonstrates high unemployment, low median income, and a high rate of poverty, then the assessable base or value of the real estate upon which taxes are calculated is low. This dictates that the local government has only a limited ability to raise taxes and thereby realize additional revenue. It may very well be that the population of this political jurisdiction cannot afford to pay additional taxes that could fund new programs.

In the case of nonprofits, financial need may be demonstrated by a statement that the organization has a small donor base or that a reduction in donations over a certain period of time has occurred. Information should also be given on the nonprofit's operating costs in order to show the amount of money that is being spent to keep the organization going.

Please refer to Appendix F, which is a sample proposal, for an example of a well-written needs statement. I cannot overemphasize the importance of taking time to gather facts that will support the need for a project. Quite often, this part of the application can be worth as much as 30 percent of the total project score.

PROJECT DESCRIPTION

As the name of this section implies, this is a straightforward statement of the activities that will take place if the application should be funded. As in the needs statement, it is best to be clear, direct, and specific. If a reviewer cannot determine what is going to be done, it is hard to rate and rank the application. In those cases, the reviewing agency will be forced to either turn the project down or, if program regulations allow, ask for additional information.

Although the needs statement is a critical piece of the application, the rest of it will not make sense unless it is clear what is going to be done. It is important to reiterate in the project description section the overall amount requested, along with the price tag for some of the major cost categories. If the grant writer is requesting funding to purchase a specific piece of equipment or several pieces of equipment, it is well to include a price quotation from two or more vendors. This price quotation will generally include specific information as to the make and model of the equipment.

A description of a proposed land purchase should include the acreage and exact location of the property, along with its eventual use. The purchase of a building should be addressed by giving a specific location, square footage, description of the interior and exterior appearance, and the types of use to which it is suitable. If the building is to be used for a specific program, the grant writer should discuss the number of persons to be served, the demographic characteristics of those persons, the type of program to be utilized, and the frequency of the services rendered.

When funds are being requested for an educational program, the project description section should clearly state the number of persons to be served, the methods by which those persons will be recruited, the content of the program, the frequency of the meetings, and the expected end result.

GOALS AND OBJECTIVES

If the needs section can best be described as answering the question "What is our current situation?" the goals and objectives section can best be described as "What is it that we hope to accomplish?" This section is critical to the success of any grant proposal. Most simple projects will have one major, overriding goal and several objectives that describe how the implementing agency will reach its goal. Complex projects will often have several goals, each with its own set of objectives.

For example, a program to provide job services and life skills training to disadvantaged individuals may have as its goal the empowering of these individuals to live independently at an economic level that sustains their needs. Objectives to reach this goal may be described as follows:

- To reach at least 50 percent of the individuals in need of this type of assistance in the target area
- To provide training in resume writing
- To bolster the self-confidence of participants so that they can go through job interviews confidently
- To teach participants how to access training appropriate for what they wish to do
- To teach participants good job search skills
- To teach participants how to manage their money effectively
- To provide training in social skills to enable trainees to act appropriately in situations involving others
- To accomplish a job placement rate of at least 80 percent of the participants
- To accomplish a job retention rate of at least 75 percent of those who receive jobs

In the above example, some of the objectives are statements of what the program plans to do, while other objectives state what the end result of the activities will be (i.e., the final two objectives). This information is requested primarily to ensure that the reviewers have a clear idea of the impact the grant money will have. Even if the application does not request this information, the applicant should know what the goals and objectives of the program will be. This exercise is helpful in organizing one's thinking to determine whether the proposed approach is the best one and tying that approach into desired outcomes.

It is important to make the goals realistic, but yet ambitious enough to let the funder know that you plan to aggressively work to accomplish those goals and objectives. Many grant applications I have seen merely recite the activities that will be undertaken. For example, a program that plans to develop a community center may list as its objectives the accomplishment of purchasing the land, tearing down an old building on the property, and building a new community center. While these are certainly steps along the way, this does not give the funder adequate information as to what difference the community center will make in the neighborhood in which it is located.

The applicant should list the various programs to be operated at the community center along with the end result of those programs. The grant writer should not be afraid to be ambitious in stating goals and objectives. Nearly every grant program I have seen does not penalize a grantee for not completely reaching every objective. Some grant writers I have talked to are afraid to give ambitious goals and objectives because of their fear that the funding agency may take the money away or make them pay back funds that have already been spent if the desired results are not achieved. The funding agencies are far more interested in a good-faith effort.

Most objectives can and should be quantified. This gives the funder a frame of reference to show the impact of the program. They can then more easily rate and rank the application against the others received. This also helps the application to be more specific. As I have said before and will certainly say again, one of the most important things any grant writer can do is to be as specific as possible all the way through the application. However, not every objective can be quantified. One example might be an aggressive law enforcement program in which one of the objectives would be an increase in the residents' feeling of safety and security. It is next to impossible to quantify that factor easily. The only way to measure it would be to collect anecdotal information from the residents and neighborhood associations. Receiving a number of positive comments would certainly affirm that this objective had been accomplished. Do not be afraid to use this as one of the important objectives of a program. In the example I have given, the feelings of the residents are one of the most important outcomes.

The following is an example of the objectives and performance measures that could be proposed in an application for a law enforcement agency to purchase equipment.

Our goal is to reduce crime in the city of Woodlawn. Objectives are as follows:

1. Decrease the number of unreported crimes
2. Increase the number of arrests by 25 percent
3. Increase the percentage of convictions by 50 percent
4. Enhance the feeling of safety and security felt by the residents of Woodlawn
5. Purchase and install a network-based digital video management system

ADMINISTRATIVE CAPACITY

Funding agencies wish to know as much as possible about their applicants. This is based upon their need to know that their funds will be in safe hands. It is their money and they do not want it to go to waste. One of the most important things you can do is to state unequivocally in this section of the application that the project will be a priority for your organization and that you commit to get the job done within the required time frame.

Grant applicants should provide the following information in this section of the application:

- brief history of the organization
- mission of the organization
- accomplishments, particularly those that bear directly on the type of activity for which funds are being requested
- experience with other grant programs, including a statement that no problems have been experienced (if this is the case)
- description of staff and how its size, expertise, and training makes the organization qualified to undertake the project
- resumes of key staff members (if requested or if the applicant thinks that it will add substantially to the application)
- a detailed explanation of who will do what

The brief history of the organization should be included in order to give the funding agency a sense of the applicant and to allow it to see at a glance how it has evolved over time. Positive past experience with other grant programs will let the funder know that it is unlikely that unpleasant problems with grant administration will crop up. Past issues with the administration of grant funds are one of the worst nightmares of any grant maker. Serious concerns arise if the grantee does not administer the program the way it was described in the application, funds are misappropriated, financial and programmatic documentation is inadequate or missing, required administrative steps are not taken, or any violation of law occurs.

If there have been problems with previous grants, it is well to say so. Word gets out fast in the grant world. If there have been issues, the grant maker will very likely find out sooner rather than later. Serious problems with previous grants will usually preclude an organization from receiving other grants for a while. This is especially true for those applicants who are applying again to the same agency that funded the previous grant. Sometimes, the "desert period" is only a year or so. I have seen it last for as much as five years. The best thing to do is to administer all grants according to program regulations and in an honest and effective manner. This saves so much time, worry, and aggravation.

However, if this does happen to you, do whatever it takes to quickly and efficiently resolve any problems with the funding agency. Being able to point to this cooperation in subsequent applications will actually earn you points. I can think of an incredible example of a nonprofit that was not thinking about the future. This particular organization "lost" all of its records pertaining to a very large federal grant.

When the federal staff arrived to do an audit, there was little or no paper trail to document what actually happened. The nonprofit was duly chastised and was told they could not qualify for funding under this very popular program for a few years. After the few years had passed, they were able to reapply and in due course received another grant. This project was implemented and completed and after a period of time, the federal staff appeared to conduct their monitoring visit. What do you suppose happened? You guessed it! They lost the files again. Needless to say, this earned them the reputation of not really caring about fulfilling their grant responsibilities.

This is the time to toot your own horn. It is not the time to be modest or self-effacing. Just as you would in a job interview or on a resume, put your very best foot forward and brag on yourself. Take the extra time to discuss the special skills and talents of key staff members, extracting from their resumes any relevant experience that will show your agency's ability to get the job done.

BUDGET

This is a critical piece to understanding your project. This section, in addition to the project description, should give a clear statement of what you plan to do. I have seen any number of applications in which it is unclear in the narrative exactly what is going to be done with the funding. This, of course, is no way to write a grant proposal. However, many grant writers seem to have difficulty in actually spelling out how the funds will be utilized.

Many state and federal applications have a specific form that must be used for the budget section. The U.S. Department of Justice, for some of its programs, requests applicants to show their costs allocated among several categories, including personnel (salaries and fringe benefit costs must be described separately), operating costs, travel, equipment, consultant costs, supplies, construction and indirect costs. This form is included as Appendix G.

Many foundation applications and applications for smaller federal and state programs do not request that the applicant fill out a particular form. The structure of the budget is therefore up to the applicant. In this case, I would recommend a very simple and straightforward format. Given below is a sample budget for an application where no specific format was given.

Overtime for Speed Limit Enforcement and Seatbelt Law Enforcement

Overtime for speed limit enforcement—750 hours @ $35 per hour = $26,250

(This overtime will be expended evenly throughout the two-year grant period)

Overtime for seatbelt law enforcement—750 hours @ $35 per hour = $26,250

(This overtime will be expended evenly throughout the two-year program period)

TOTAL: $52,500
Two grant-related meetings:

Meeting in Washington, DC—two staff members @ $375 = $750
Meeting within the region—two staff members @ $375 = $750

TOTAL: $1,500
GRAND TOTAL: $54,000

Notes: We are within driving distance of Washington, DC, and within driving distance of any city in the region at which the second meeting could be held. We are therefore budgeting $110 per trip for transportation costs and assume that both staff members would be traveling together. We have assumed that each meeting would last two days. Our budget for meals is $85 per staff member per day, for a grand total of $680 for the two meetings. We are also allowing $150 per night for four nights of lodging for these two meetings.

Most applications require that the budget itself be accompanied by a brief narrative that provides additional detail that is not obvious in the budget itself. This is the place to give a more detailed description of any equipment that is to be purchased with the grant. I would recommend using the narrative to provide information about the make, model number, manufacturer and vendor. However, it is not necessary to write more than a few sentences. In some cases, funding agencies request that applicants reiterate the purpose of the equipment. When describing supplies, it is best to itemize as much as possible, even though this may be somewhat tedious. The grant writer should put as few items as possible in the "miscellaneous" category.

As an example, let us assume that a nonprofit agency is applying for funding to pay one year's salary and fringe benefits for a program officer. The total requested is $50,000. A good budget narrative is as follows:

> The $50,000 requested will pay the salary and fringe benefit costs for one year for a program officer who will be dedicated to implementing our anti-drug education program. This position will be filled from outside the agency by an individual who has experience with both youth and drug resistance programs. This individual will also have good communication skills, some knowledge of the commonly used drugs in the area, and the ability to teach others the benefits of abstinence from drugs. Of the amount requested, $40,000 will be dedicated to salary and the remaining $10,000 will be allocated to fringe benefit costs. This represents an hourly rate of $19.00 for a 40-hour week. The $10,000 in fringe benefit costs will be allocated as follows: $4,000 for health insurance, $2,000 for retirement, $100 for life insurance, $2,500 for Social Security and Medicare, $700 for vacation, and $700 for sick leave.

An example of a good budget narrative for a construction project is as follows:

> Our agency is requesting $250,000 to construct a new multipurpose building on our site at Wayne and Cedar Streets in Moncton. This building will be used for athletic activities, cultural activities, meetings, and social events. It will include a commercial kitchen, a gym, and an auditorium with a stage. The new center is expected to serve approximately 2,000 persons per year. The building will be 5,000 square feet in area, with a construction cost of approximately $50 per square foot. Please find attached a detailed architect's cost estimate.

Appendix G provides sufficient detail to guide the grant writer in thoroughly and correctly documenting the items requested in the budget.

SUSTAINABILITY

Funding agencies want to know how the project will be continued once the grant has expired. Most programs require that the grantee spend the funds within a specified period of time, usually one to two years. This is often a very difficult section to write. Most applicants are not able to identify a ready source of cash to continue the program. If they did, they would not need grant funding. If they do not have the funds when they file the application, they are not likely to have them at some future date.

Most applicants therefore really have no idea where they will get the money to continue a program. It is wise to not make grandiose claims in this section, such as saying that the applicant organization will fund the program out of its own budget at the expiration of the grant, not expecting anyone to check whether this was actually done. Information about which agencies make false claims will get around. It is better to simply say that you will look into this rather than making statements that you know you cannot stand by.

It is okay to say that the applicant organization will *consider* funding this out of its own budget. It is entirely possible that the fiscal situation will have changed in a year or two. Applicants may also say that they will look for grant funds from other sources,

EVALUATION PLAN

Even if this were not required by the funding agencies, evaluating the success of your project makes sense. Obviously, if a significant amount of funds are poured into a particular project and the end results are not what had been hoped for, it is time to change strategies. It would be interesting to see how many applicants would propose an evaluation plan if the funding agency did not request it. It is doubtful that all applicants would want to go through the extra steps. The main reason for this, in my opinion, is that these applicants feel that it is obvious that their approach is going to do some good. In some cases, this is correct. However, there are often many cases where a program evaluator would see some surprising results, with the project either not working at all or not working to the extent expected.

In any event, nearly every governmental or private funding agency requires some sort of documentation as to the effectiveness of the project. Put quite simply, the applicant is expected to take baseline data (statistics in effect prior to the advent of the project) and compare it to similar data once the project is complete. Often times, the full effect of a project is not noticeable until the end of the one- to two-year project period. Notwithstanding, some funding agencies will require that assessments be made every quarter.

I will give a brief example of an evaluation plan that will effectively show the success of a particular project. Let us assume that funding has been received to pay the costs of hiring teachers for an afterschool program aimed at youth at high risk of dropping out of high school. The goal of the project would be to reduce the dropout rate by 25 percent at a particular school. Project success is relatively easy to measure in this case. School administrators would calculate the dropout rate for the previous school year. This is relatively easy to do as most school districts routinely keep this information anyway. The applicant would state that the dropout rate will then be calculated for the year that the program is ongoing.

At the end of that year, the dropout rate would be compared to the dropout rate from the baseline year. A more rigorous evaluation plan would call for a system to take into account other factors besides the afterschool program. In most cases, the underlying conditions will remain generally the same, thus allowing for the premise that the after-school program is solely responsible for any decrease in the dropout rate. However, there may be other factors during the one-year period that would skew the results. In other words, the dropout rate may be affected by factors other than the afterschool program. Some of these other factors may be as follows: unusual weather conditions that cause the school (and therefore the afterschool program) to be closed more often than usual, unexpected illnesses to a greater degree than usual among the student body, transfer or resignation of a few very effective teachers, economic disruptions such as plant closings and economic recession, or a host of other factors.

Very few grantees have the sophistication necessary to quantify other factors that may have had an impact on the dropout rate. Most evaluations therefore only consider the impact of the project on a particular problem. In most cases, this is sufficient. The funding agency does not expect a scientific analysis. It is common sense that extra time spent with at-risk youth will result in improved grades and a greater desire to remain in school. Most projects, like this example, are relatively simple to measure.

Chapter Ten

Grant Administration

HOW HARD IS THIS GOING TO BE?

The grantee should be prepared for many varying requirements in grant administration. I feel that it would be helpful to give a few examples showing the difference in the required paperwork for various granting agencies. All funding agencies will request documentation that the funds were spent appropriately and for the purposes specified in the grant application. This is the very least that one can expect in terms of documentation.

Probably the simplest grants to administer are those from private foundations. The application forms can be very simple, sometimes involving no more than two pages. Sometimes, no grant agreement is required. The grantee is still obligated to use the funds for the purpose for which they were intended. I am aware of any foundation or government agencies that would simply send the money and not require some accountability.

Some foundations require several progress reports. It is also possible that special conditions may be attached to the grant in order to meet the specific preferences of the board members. These can vary widely. It may be that the foundation requires the grantee to only utilize American labor and products, or limits funding to certain geographic areas, or wishes to remain anonymous.

Most governmental entities will require the following once the grant is approved:

- Environmental review (this is sometimes done prior to approval)
- Execution of the grant agreement

- Documentation of banking information in order to expedite the processing of payments
- Written progress reports at varying intervals—these could be either quarterly, semiannually, or annually
- Execution of grant closeout documents

I have used the example of the Community Development Block Grant (CDBG) program throughout this book. This is a program with complex administrative requirements. In addition to the above, a grantee will need to undertake the following additional administrative steps with a CDBG grant:

- Prepare plans to cover the following topics—these are basically step-by-step guides as to how the jurisdiction will meet CDBG requirements in these areas:

    1. Affirmative Action Plan
    2. Minority Business Enterprise Plan
    3. Fair Housing Plan
    4. Retention of Records Plan
    5. Personnel Policy
    6. Section 504 Plan to cover issues related to services to handicapped citizens
    7. Procurement Policy

- Follow detailed labor standards steps to include the following:

    1. Insert equal opportunity clauses in the advertisement for bids.
    2. Insert equal opportunity regulations in the bid package.
    3. Conduct a preconstruction conference to explain the various CDBG labor standards requirements.
    4. Check to ensure that the contractor pays employees the required wages under the Davis-Bacon Act and review weekly payrolls.
    5. Conduct site interviews with employees to ensure that they are being paid appropriately.
    6. Hold exit interviews with the contractor to ensure that he or she has taken adequate steps to obtain the services of local, female, and minority subcontractors and suppliers.

This is the most complex set of administrative requirements of which I am aware. Indeed, most CDBG grants include funds for both general and project administration in recognition of the fact that following the requirements is a time-consuming process. Up to 15 percent of the total grant amount may be dedicated to general administration, which involves the overseeing of requirements that are not involved in actually implementing the project. This would include the environmental review, preparation of plans, and setting up the financial recordkeeping.

There is no limit on the amount of project administration funds that may be included in the grant. This would include architectural or engineering fees, as well as the time of the local grant administrator. The tasks involved in project administration are those that actually serve to move the project forward. This would include bidding, project inspection, and monitoring of project progress.

The reader can now see that there is a wide range of administrative requirements for grants, going all the way from writing one very simple report for a private foundation to the CDBG requirements. In the following sections, I will go over the various common steps in implementing a successful grant.

THE GRANT AGREEMENT

This applies mostly to government grants. Some foundations do not have a requirement for a special document to cover the grantee's responsibilities. Legally, it is assumed that the representations made in the grant application constitute the grantee's agreement to carry out the project as stated. In general, most foundations that require a grant agreement draw up very simple documents. The major reason for this is that they are not bound by federal and state law to certain requirements. It is their money, and they can do what they wish with it.

Grant agreements can vary in length from the 2 to 4 pages required by the U.S. Environmental Protection Agency all the way up to the 30 or 40 pages of a CDBG grant agreement. Because the administrative and fiscal requirements are generally the same from grant to grant, much of the governmental grant agreement is boilerplate material, with information specific to a particular grant inserted in the appropriate places.

If the grantee is a local government, the chief elected official is the person designated to sign the agreement. If a nonprofit is the grantee, generally the president of the Board of Directors is the official empowered to sign. It is a good idea to review the agreement carefully prior to signing. Most grantees have their attorney review it. I have only seen two or three grantees who decided to not proceed with the project after reading the grant agreement. Most of the provisions of the agreement relate to administering the project according to the laws governing that particular program. In addition, the grantee is signing off that the project will proceed just as it was described in the grant application.

For example, an economic development project may have been described in the application as one that would provide a certain number of jobs targeted to low- and moderate-income persons. The grant agreement is the means by which the grantee becomes legally bound to ensure that the project does indeed provide at least as many jobs as promised. In addition, the grant agreement will contain the requirements for documenting that these jobs were in fact provided.

Standard information included in the grant agreement is as follows:

- A description of the project with the amount of the grant and the amount of the local match
- Contact information for the agency and the grantee
- Grant period or timeframe by which the project must be started and deadline by which it must be completed—this is generally at least one year. However, some programs offer multiyear funding. The timeframe will be spelled out in the grant solicitation. In general, most multiyear grants provide for no more than three or four years.
- Listing of any information that the grantee must provide to the funding agency prior to beginning the project
- Information regarding the penalties to be incurred if the grant terms are not adhered to
- Provisions for modifying the project
- Listing and description of the various laws that govern the program, including those dealing with environmental review, labor standards, historic preservation, fair housing, and equal opportunity

Once the grantee is satisfied that the requirements of the grant agreement are fully understood, it should be signed and returned to the agency. It is best to complete this process as soon as possible because the project cannot start until the grant agreement is fully executed—meaning that it is signed by both the funding agency and the grantee.

ENVIRONMENTAL REVIEW

This issue must be addressed for every project for which federal funds are granted. The individual federal agencies have latitude as to when this information must be submitted. The requirement for an environmental review is derived from the National Environmental Protection Act (NEPA). This law went into effect in 1970. Like many issues that appear to be complex, the entire environmental review can be boiled down to one simple fact. The federal government wants to know whether a particular project will have an adverse impact upon the social, physical, or natural environment.

The social environment refers to quality-of-life issues that affect human society. An example of this might be a housing project that will displace low- and moderate-income families. Although the project would not be funded without including money for adequate compensation for these properties, the residents to be displaced will still experience an upheaval in their lives. They will be forced to leave familiar neighborhoods with familiar faces and all that implies. The idea of "home" is more than just a physical one. To the credit of the federal government, this type of issue is taken into account in environmental reviews. Many novice grant writers are surprised that this factor would be part of the equation in this type of review because most people automatically think of the "environment" as being strictly natural resources, such as rivers, lakes, streams, forests, and mountains.

The physical environment refers to man-made structures. As an example, Form RD 1940–20 (Request for Environmental Information), used by the U.S. Department of Agriculture (USDA), asks whether a particular project will have an impact on the following man-made facilities: industrial, commercial, residential, agricultural, grazing land, mining, recreational facilities, transportation, parks, hospitals, schools, historical sites, and solid waste management.

An example is given here to help the reader understand how this issue should be addressed. A nonprofit agency may wish to apply for funds to construct a play area in the central business district of a city. The district obviously contains commercial shops and may contain a subway system or a bus line as well as hospitals and schools. Form RD 1940–20 would require that the applicant state whether the project would have an effect on those shops, transportation facilities, hospitals, and schools or be located in an area that contained those types of entities. This form also requires that the applicant provide a brief narrative discussing how the project would affect those aspects of the physical environment.

The third type of environment, the natural environment, refers to features of geography and wildlife that most of us think of as comprising "nature." Form RD 1940–20 separates these into categories as follows: forests, aquifer recharge area, steep slopes, wildlife refuge, shoreline, beaches, dunes, estuary, wetlands, floodplain, wilderness, wild and scenic rivers, critical habitat, wildlife, air quality, energy supplies, and coastal barrier resources systems. The federal government offers guidance as to exactly how each term is defined. This guidance is intended to assist the applicant in deciding whether a particular natural structure fits the federal definition.

USDA requires that a substantial amount of environmental review information be submitted with the preapplication for a number of their programs. An additional environmental review is performed by USDA staff if the application is approved. Other agencies, such as the Economic Development Administration of the U.S. Department of Commerce, require that the applicant address environmental issues only briefly in the application. In some cases, all that may be required is simply a statement that the project will not cause any adverse impact upon the environment. Then, once the application is approved, a more lengthy review is completed, either by the federal agency staff or by the successful applicant.

Some programs, such as the Small Cities Community Development Block Grant Program, do not require that environmental issues be addressed at all in the application. However, successful applicants must complete the environmental review process prior to funds being released. This program puts the entire burden upon the grantee rather than the funding agency. The grantee will complete the paperwork and submit it to the appropriate state agency administering the program. This involves filling out a number of forms and placing a notice in a local newspaper addressing the level of environmental review that was undertaken, the effect on the environment, the availability of the environmental review record to the public, and the deadline for public comment.

There are three categories of findings. A project may be "exempt," meaning just that. Most of the forms would not need to be completed. This would generally occur in the case of funding for studies and preliminary engineering reports, projects for which no physical activity would take place. At this point, it is considered irrelevant that the studies may eventually lead to a physical project. If the physical project itself is funded, a more comprehensive environment review would take place at that point.

The second type of finding would be "categorically excluded." This type of project would still require the filing of a number of environment review forms and the publication of a notice. Categorically excluded projects are primarily those in which rehabilitation or repair would take place on existing facilities, rather than the construction of new facilities. Additionally, in order to be considered in this category, a project must not change the use of a facility and not increase its density by more than 20 percent.

The final type of project, one that involves major new construction or a significant change in the environment, requires a full environmental assessment. As the reader can imagine, this is the most complex type of environmental review. Even so, the assessment does not need to be lengthy. I have completed approved environmental assessments of only 10 pages. These assessments must be very tightly written and address all of the pertinent and applicable facts in a very simple and direct manner. It is not necessary to use a lot of "filler" or overly flowery language.

FINANCIAL RECORDKEEPING

One does not have to be a top expert in grant writing to know that keeping track of the finances is extremely important. This is the front line of all administrative duties. The funding agencies need to know that the money they are giving the grantee will be spent on the project for which it was intended, in the way in which it was described in the grant application, and that the records will be kept so as to allow an auditor or reviewer to easily see how and when the funds were spent.

Most private foundations do not require the sophisticated and time-consuming financial recordkeeping methods that government agencies do. It is often adequate to maintain only the following: evidence of deposit of the check, evidence of disbursement, and evidence that the services paid for were provided. The grantee is often permitted to utilize existing accounts and bookkeeping methods in order to keep these very simple records.

More sophisticated recordkeeping is required for federal and state government grants. I will use the example of a law enforcement agency that has received a grant for equipment. Once the equipment has been ordered and received, a financial obligation is generated in the form of an invoice. In most cases, it is necessary to incur the obligation prior to drawing any funds. In our hypothetical example, the grant only allows for drawing funds once every quarter. The funding agency has specific forms that must be used to request funds and to report the status of grant monies. The reporting quarters are as follows: January 1–March 31, April 1–June 30, July 1–September 30, and October 1–December 31.

The financial forms must be submitted within 15 days after the end of each quarter. The documentation of the spending does not need to accompany the request for funds, although the grantee is liable for this information if the funding agency should ever audit the grant.

This example represents just one common methodology for requesting funds. Many grant programs permit the grantee to draw funds whenever they wish. There may sometimes be limitations to the number of draws that may be made within a certain timeframe, or there may be a specified minimum draw amount. For example, one popular federal program only allows the grantee to draw funds once per month.

The granting agency will let you know when the documentation of expenses must be submitted with a draw form. In my experience, approximately 75 percent of grant programs require that this documentation be provided.

In general, most federal and state programs disperse funds within 30 days after the draw form is submitted. It is very rare to see a faster turnaround than that. Automatic deposits are becoming the norm now. Many of the smaller municipalities, counties, and nonprofits that I have dealt with over the years have had grant funds deposited into their existing general account. More often than not, granting agencies do not require that a separate account be established for grant funds.

Most of the municipalities that I work with are small and do not have the capacity to front the money for a large project. In these cases, the funding agency allows for advance payments. This is critical for large projects such as water and sewer work, where even a small community of 2,000 persons can have a sewer project costing $5 million or more.

My advice is to learn up front what the financial recordkeeping requirements are and follow them precisely. Be sure to keep records that will adequately reflect when the money came in, when it went out, and to whom it was sent.

LABOR STANDARDS

Federally funded projects that involve construction or rehabilitation require that the contractor be chosen in an open and competitive manner and that certain wage rates be paid to workers on the project. Wage rates are governed by the Davis-Bacon Act. This law also requires that workers on federally funded jobs be paid one and a half times their normal hourly rate for all hours worked in excess of 40 within a given week. The U.S. Department of Labor Web site states that the Davis-Bacon Act applies to "all contractors and subcontractors on federally-funded or assisted contracts in excess of $2,000 for the construction, alteration or repair (including painting and decorating) of public buildings or public works."

Prior to soliciting bids, the grantee must request a "wage decision" from either the U.S. Department of Labor or the state agency that is charged with administering the federal funds. The requester must delineate the types of workers that will be needed. The decision will list the various trades in certain categories of work—that is, highway, heavy construction, water and sewer, or another classification, along with the applicable minimum wage rates and required fringe benefits for each job classification. The wage decision will also specify the geographical area and period of time in which it is effective.

The successful bidder must sign a document agreeing to pay no less than the Davis-Bacon wage rate to the workers on the project and to submit payroll forms on a weekly basis. These forms list the worker, his address and Social Security number, job classification, hourly wage, total pay for the week, and deductions. Some programs require that the grant administrator visit the job site to interview workers in order to determine whether the provisions of the Act are being carried out. The interviewer will determine whether the workers are actually performing the job classifications they are listed as performing, are being paid the wage rate appropriate to their position, are being paid for overtime, and are not being asked to "kick back" part of their wages to their employer.

Grantees may be asked to monitor the contractor's performance in regard to the Affirmative Action and Disadvantaged Business Enterprise (DBE) laws and regulations as well as the requirements of Section 3 of the Housing and Urban Development Act of 1968. The latter law requires that contractors make a good-faith effort to hire any new workers needed for the project or buy supplies and materials from among the individuals and businesses in the "project area." In rural areas, the project area may be the entire county, while in more urbanized areas, it may be a particular city. This term is somewhat loosely defined, and it is best to check with the funding agency for its definition as it relates to your grant.

Labor standards for federally funded projects are very complex and could cover an entire book in itself. I would like to stress here the importance of finding out which regulations apply to your project and then being conscientious about following them every step of the way. If this is not done, the grantee may be placed in the costly and embarrassing situation of having to repay the funding provided to them under the grant. I am familiar with one county that had to repay $150,000 because they did not follow these regulations.

As a grant consultant, one of my major jobs, other than to procure grant money for my clients, is to ensure that they never have to repay any funds. This involves being proactive, timely, and assertive. Do not let a contractor intimidate you into not performing your role as a monitor of labor standards. If this should happen, I guarantee you that everyone will be sorry later on.

I will give an example that illustrates the importance of aggressively enforcing these provisions. A particular state recently awarded a grant to a city to undertake a facade improvement program limited to the downtown area, with the goal of attracting additional businesses to the downtown that would help to raise the low economic indicators of the area. The businesses, the city, and the residents all stood to benefit.

The state officials involved in approving this grant were likewise anxious to bring this project to fruition. They fast tracked the approval and made an exception to their usual rules by allowing the city to start spending the funds immediately, even prior to receiving the grant agreement. There was a miscommunication that resulted in the individual businesses entering into a contract for their projects, when this would normally be the prerogative of the grantee—the city. To make matters even worse, the individual shops were not aware that their contractors had to pay Davis-Bacon wages.

The city's grant administrator finally became aware of the problem .What followed next was the torturous process of undoing all that had been done and starting from the beginning in order to ensure that the applicable laws were followed. There is no escaping the fact that these laws must be followed. True, the steps involved can sometimes be onerous. However, it is best to just move forward and get the job done rather than worrying about how much work it is going to be. The point here is to insist upon doing the right thing, rather than the easy thing.

PERFORMANCE REPORTS

As the name implies, performance reports are no more and no less than a description of what has happened with the grant project to date. For a foundation, it can be as simple as a two-paragraph description, along with an accounting of the funds.

The same principle applies for government funding. This is the "who, what, where, and when" of the grant world. A very complicated performance report could be as much as 10 to 15 pages and cover the following information:

- Amount of funds spent during the reporting period, separated into the grant amount and the match amount
- Amount of grant and match funds spent since the beginning of the project
- Narrative description of what has physically occurred during the reporting period
- Listing of all contracts awarded during the subject period, including the name of the contractor, address, employer ID number, amount of the contract, date of the award, and whether the contractor is considered to be a Disadvantaged Business Enterprise
- Listing of accomplishments by unit—that is, number of houses rehabilitated, linear feet of street work completed, number of brochures printed and distributed, number of educational events held, along with a percentage of the total the accomplishment represents.
- Numeric description of the beneficiaries assisted—this may include demographic information such as gender, ethnicity, age, and disabled status
- If new jobs are involved, the number of jobs provided, along with the number provided to low- and moderate-income persons, the job classification, and the average wage
- Status of any special requirements, such as environmental review or historic preservation documentation

I have never seen an agency that requires reporting more often than once per quarter. Most reports are required to be submitted every six months or once a year.

RETENTION OF RECORDS

Most funding agencies require that records be maintained for at least three years following the end of the project. I have always been very conservative in my advice to clients, and have recommended that these records not be destroyed at all.

The reason for this retention of records is that if any issues should be raised about the administration of the grant, the funding agency needs to have access to records that can prove or disprove the issues. It is therefore in the grantee's best interest to save the records for as long as possible so that the fact that the project was administered in a proper manner can be proven.

I make these recommendations out of an abundance of caution. This policy has enabled my clients to avoid having any monitoring issues or allegations of improper administration.

As a consultant, I have learned the importance of maintaining duplicate sets of records with my office maintaining one set and the client retaining the other set. Most funding agencies are not comfortable with a consulting administrator having possession of the sole set of records pertaining to a grant. An example with which I am familiar will serve to illustrate the importance of duplicate sets of records. A small town had completed a very ambitious construction project that was funded by a state agency. Grantees of this program can expect to have their projects monitored at some point after completion. However, when it came time for the monitoring visit, the town could not find their records anywhere. This is not completely unheard of in very small communities with a limited staff and inadequate time to properly categorize, label, and store files. It was very fortunate that their grant consultant had a duplicate set of records that could be used for the visit, which is described in more detail below.

MONITORING VISITS

Some agencies will perform a review (monitoring visit) of the grantee's files after the grant period has expired. The purpose of this review is to determine whether the grantee carried out all of its administrative and financial responsibilities in an acceptable manner. Among the items generally covered in such a review are the following:

- If a public hearing was required, did the grantee hold the hearing, provide ample advance notice to the public, and retain documentation of what transpired?
- Was any competitive bidding handled in a fair and equitable manner, with ample opportunity given to any Disadvantaged Business Enterprise?
- Was the work to be funded by the agency properly inspected prior to any disbursements of funds?
- Were all financial transactions completely documented and properly handled consistent with the policies of both the grantee and the funding agency?
- If the project involved direct assistance limited to individuals with certain characteristics—that is, low- and moderate-income status—did the grantee properly qualify each beneficiary?
- Were project goals and objectives met?
- Did the grantee evaluate the project for its success in meeting the identified need?

Some programs monitor every grant. It may even take a period of a few years after the expiration of the grant, depending on staff, but the monitoring will be done. Other agencies monitor only a small percentage of their grants on a random basis. Still others send in the monitoring team only when there is reason to suspect there are problems.

Most monitoring visits of which I am aware are done in the spirit of trying to assist the grantee. Naturally, if problems are found, corrective action must be taken. However, most funding agencies tend to take the attitude that the monitoring visit is more of a technical assistance session. However, if monies are spent improperly, either on purpose or inadvertently, the grantee must generally repay the entire amount in question. One example of this would be a grantee that did not properly qualify certain individual beneficiaries of assistance. If this were the case, they would generally have to repay the amount of direct assistance provided to persons who did not qualify under the guidelines of the program.

A couple of examples will help to put into perspective the natural stresses and strains associated with being reviewed by a federal or state agency. Many people feel that their self-worth is on the line in a review of this nature, despite the fact that there are often things beyond the control of the individual that have a bearing on how the grant is administered. These examples will show how it is possible to go from great angst to sailing through the challenges of the monitoring visit.

When I was working for the city of Salisbury before I started my consulting business, the U.S. Department of Housing and Urban Development was administering the CDBG program. They sent a team of four people down from Baltimore for a period of four days in order to review three grants. When the review came out, it was generally favorable, with only a few very minor suggestions for change. However, this whole incident caused me a great deal of stress because it was the first review I had ever undergone. I laugh now when I think about how long I felt stressed about this review before, during, and after. This was much wasted effort.

Very soon after I became a consultant, I faced another review, again for the CDBG program. This was a two-day deal, again with numerous staff members, and if anything, even more angst on my part than the previous review. However, there was a very good reason for this. As an employee, I felt that there was some margin for error. As a consultant, I felt that I had to be perfect and that any findings at all would reflect poorly on my status as an "expert." I worked very hard to make sure all was in order. No findings were made. Now, a monitoring visit is no big deal to me at all. I literally experience no sense of stress.

To wrap up this chapter, I will first give the reasoning behind these monitoring visits and then give some general advice to the grantee on how to weather them. For the most part, these visits are made by staff that is not invested in finding problems. To the contrary, my experience has been that the reviewers much prefer to find that the grantees are doing a good job. I realize that this sounds simplistic, but I am trying to make the point that most reviewers are not "control freaks" who like to cause problems. They are there because the regulations of the program mandate that they be there. I must also say that going into the field often gives the staff a welcome break from the everyday office routine and gives them a chance to look at interesting projects in new places. This naturally dictates that they are feeling in a positive frame of mind.

The following is my best advice to you on how to prepare for and weather a monitoring visit:

- Be sure to review the files closely beforehand, but do not become obsessed with relatively minor matters.
- Realize that if you have done your job all along, the monitoring visit will be relatively easy.
- In responding to the agency's request for a specific date, be flexible and do not try to put it off—this will make the agency wonder if there is some very good reason why you do not want the visit to occur.
- Be courteous and polite to the reviewers—be your natural self.
- Realize that this review could help you to become a better grant administrator.
- If there are findings, respond promptly and completely—the agency will be much more likely to clear the record as quickly as possible.
- Learn from the experience—use it to help administer the next grant even more professionally.

I realize that the information presented in this chapter points up the sometimes complicated nature of grant administration. However, with experience and dedication, the grant writer can learn how to effectively administer grant funds in a short amount of time. I cannot stress enough the necessity of being in close contact with the funding agency. They are happy to help. It is to their advantage that the grant funds are administered correctly so that future monitoring visits will not be fraught with problems. The benefit of receiving grant funds to alleviate a serious need far outweighs the sometimes cumbersome steps involved in grant administration.

Chapter Eleven

What to Do If the Grant Application Is Not Approved

REASONS FOR REJECTION

This would be a good place to review the many and various reasons for rejection of an application. Some of these are as follows:

- The grant proposal is poorly written.
- The project is a poor fit with the need and will not do much to alleviate that need.
- The proposed activities are not clearly thought out and do not seem feasible.
- The competition from other applications is overwhelming.
- The application is good and the need is great, but other projects will serve even needier populations.
- The funding agency does not have confidence that the applicant has the capacity to successfully carry out the project.
- The applicant has had problems in administering other grants.

Part of the problem is getting to the real root of the rejection. This can sometimes be difficult, as discussed in this chapter.

REQUESTING A DEBRIEFING FROM THE FUNDING AGENCY OR FOUNDATION

I will discuss receiving debriefings from governmental agencies separately from private foundations because there is a world of difference in what to expect. A debriefing is a discussion with the funding agency as to why the application was not funded. Many governmental agencies are happy to discuss the reasons for rejection; however, I would urge the grant writer to listen to the debriefings with a bit of caution. Feedback is sometimes given by staff members who were not actually reviewers and were not charged with the responsibility of assigning points to the application. When this is the case, something can sometimes get lost in the translation.

Overall, however, it is an excellent idea to request a debriefing. This information can be invaluable in developing the proposal for a resubmittal or for a submittal to a different agency. This is especially true for beginning grant writers. As one gains more and more experience, it will be easier to see the weaknesses in your proposal even prior to submittal. I would definitely recommend that a proposal still be resubmitted even though there are minor flaws in it. Sometimes these can be worked out with the funding agency. Sometimes they are so insignificant as not to matter. It is important to take to heart the information received in a debriefing and attempt to remedy the problems identified.

In my experience, I have found 90 percent of funding agency officials to be extremely helpful and willing to work with the applicants in order to strengthen the proposal. However, it is sad but true that once in a while the grant writer will come up against an agency official who appears to overly enjoy the feeling of power that comes with dispensing funds. In the few cases of this type that I have seen, the person misuses their position to make the applicants feel miserable and totally insignificant. Debriefings from this sort of individual are rarely useful. I have seen situations where they put applicants through unnecessary hoops in order to satisfy their need to control others.

This issue needs to be discussed so that aspiring and even experienced grant writers can deal with it if it should become necessary. The best thing to do when encountering an individual such as this is to listen carefully, take notes, and then sift out what seems to be useful advice from less than useful advice. If at all possible, contact a second individual at the same agency in order to check the information. If these officials become unduly demanding, I have found that the best policy is to stand up for yourself. This can be done pleasantly but firmly. I know that this is difficult to do when certain individuals have the approval authority over your grant money. However, this yields positive results over the long run, as these types of officials tend to be attracted to those that they think they can bully.

In summation, my advice regarding debriefings is very simple. Try to the best of your ability to follow the advice of the funding agency. Change the application and/or the structure of the project if advised to do so and if you feel that this can be done without compromising your good intentions. Some of the advice you may receive in a debriefing is as follows:

- More detail needs to be provided in the application.
- A required component of the application is missing.
- Not enough matching funds are being provided.
- The grant writer did not follow program regulations and guidelines in developing the application.
- Required documentation was not submitted.

An example shows how the applicants can receive conflicting advice from different staff members at the same agency. What is even more distressing is that sometimes the same staff member can give applicants different advice from year to year. I was told the story about a historic district in another part of the country that had applied for a historic district designation. The application was turned down. This was a particularly prestigious designation that was administered by the state on behalf of the federal government. The state officials were charged with working with applicants during the preparation of the application. They would then make comments on the submissions and pass the applications on to the federal agency for a final decision.

The first time the historic district commission applied for this designation, they were rejected. They were told that they did not have "a story to tell." From talking with other people in the area who are familiar with the historic district, this was far from the truth. A number of other negative comments were made, including the fact that they did not have promotional material.

The following year, the state staff strongly encouraged them to apply and, in fact, was quite proactive in pressuring the organization to submit an application. However, one of the comments made by one of the historic district board members was that if the reviewers thought there had been no story to tell before, then nothing had happened in the meantime to change this. Several of the board members did not want to submit an application for this reason. However, the state staff still pressed the group to apply. Either they were giving poor advice to the commission, or the initial review comment was totally wrong and would be reversed the next time.

The application was again turned down. This is a prime example of how things can sometimes get lost in the translation. In my experience, when the state is the initial point of review for a federal agency, there is sometimes some confusion as to what the federal agency really wants. I have seen a number of situations where this has not been adequately relayed by the federal agency to state governments. In many cases, the state staff is doing the best they can, but some of their advice to applicants is primarily guesswork.

Foundations are not as likely to give debriefings. I have heard from numerous nonprofits that they are sometimes not even notified that their grant has been turned down. In other instances, when a letter is sent, it often does not give a reason for rejection. I would still advise applicants to attempt to receive a debriefing from private foundations. However, I would caution you not to be too optimistic about the foundation staff members being willing to take the time to provide this information.

One of the major reasons for this is that governmental funders are more or less required to respond to applicants due to the fact that they are public agencies. This implies an obligation on their part to be responsive to the public. Foundations are not under this sort of obligation. Many times, these are family funds that are given only to projects that meet their very clearly specified interests. These foundations are freer to pick and choose without regard to a specific rating and ranking system. They do not have the obligations that go with being a public agency and can be as private as they wish.

PUTTING THE REJECTION INTO PERSPECTIVE

Most grant writers tend to blame themselves unduly if an application is rejected. Granted, there are sometimes instances where obvious mistakes have been made on the part of the grant writer. However, I have found that most professionals in this field are sincerely dedicated to their jobs and really want to receive the grant money. This is a very big incentive to do the very best job possible on the grant application.

This field of work has some features that are different from many others. There is a need to remain focused and stay on track, as tangible products must be produced. It is hard to "slack off" when there is a submission deadline to be met. The funding agencies will not accept late applications. Grant writers who do not produce an application on time will not have many more chances to redeem themselves. Not meeting the deadline and, therefore, not being able to submit an application is considered to be a failure of the worst sort.

This of course produces a pressure to perform, which can, in extreme cases, induce performance anxiety. This is exacerbated by the highly competitive field in which the grant writer operates. In the case of most federal and state grant opportunities, all municipalities, counties, or nonprofits applying are in competition with one another. This does nothing to reduce the pressure.

Conversely, when an application is approved, the grant writer becomes a "rainmaker." As one can imagine, this is a highly respected person who is given a great deal of importance within the organization.

The purpose of saying all of this is to caution the grant writer to not become overly identified with the results of any one particular application or even several applications. In order to preserve one's sense of balance, it is necessary to not become overly dejected when an application is not funded or to take too much of the credit for successful applications.

UNDERSTANDING SUCCESS RATIOS AND HOW THEY VARY FROM PROGRAM TO PROGRAM

In discussing this issue, I am reminded of situations where, just when one thinks that there are rules that define all situations, numerous exceptions are found. The simple answer here is that success ratios vary widely from program to program. One example of a program that tries to fund as many applications as possible is the Community Facilities program administered by the U.S. Department of Agriculture. This program provides funds for capital and equipment costs for essential services such as health care and law enforcement. These applications are accepted on a continuous basis throughout the year. Some grant requests may have to wait until the following program year, but in general, the agency is able to fund at least part of the request for many of the applications.

Some state-funded programs likewise fund as many applications as possible, but at a lower level than the amount requested. For example, I am familiar with a state agency that is charged with dispensing both federal and state funds for law enforcement purposes. Probably at least 50 percent of the applications get funded. However, an applicant requesting overtime monies may only receive half of the amount that they have applied for. Another agency requesting 10 in-car video cameras may only receive funding for 5.

A grant writer may eventually see over time what the success ratios are with various programs. It also helps to discuss this with your peers who have also submitted applications to the same program. Most governmental agencies publish the complete list of projects that have been funded as well as the amount of funding awarded. There is no doubt that this field is extremely competitive, but there is a wide variation in success ratios from program to program and agency to agency. In general, many national competitions are much more competitive than state-funded programs. Although there is obviously a much higher amount of funding available, opening the field up wider naturally decreases the success ratio. This is therefore a very important part of the equation.

Two examples may serve to help the reader understand just how competitive some of these programs are. One of my clients recently received funding to retain two law enforcement officers that were due to be laid off as a result of the deteriorating economy. This funding was provided by the U.S. Justice Department under the Cops Hiring Program. This application was one of only seven approved in the entire state. In announcing these awards, the Justice Department noted that they had received applications requesting seven times as much money as was available.

I wrote another successful application to the appropriate state agency administering American Recovery and Reinvestment Act monies in early 2009 for a water and sewer project. Funding was only available to cover 3 percent of the dollars requested by local governments. This and the previous examples show how long the odds can be sometimes. However, I would encourage the grant writer to not be dismayed by this situation. Just forge ahead and make the application as well-written and well-documented as you possibly can. This may sound as if I am encouraging grant writers to routinely waste their time on applications that have very little chance of being funded. What I am really saying is that the grant writer should be aware of the success ratios but should not let that be the sole factor in deciding whether to submit an application.

This concern is more pressing if an organization is paying a significant amount of money to a consultant to write grant applications. It is the responsibility of the consultant to fully inform the client of the chances of being funded so that the organization can make the judgment as to whether it is worth the time and money involved. Most of my clients have been with me for a number of years and, therefore, are well aware of how these ratios work. However, I am always careful to let them know when the chances are very small and give them all the information they need to decide whether they wish to pay my fee to write and submit the application.

WHEN YOU SHOULD REAPPLY TO THE SAME AGENCY OR FOUNDATION

The quick answer here is to first check to see whether the funding agency or foundation allows resubmissions at a later date or imposes a minimum amount of time before the application can be resubmitted. I am hard-pressed to think of any cases where there is a complete prohibition on resubmitting a particular project. Many foundations will not allow successful applicants to apply for another project until a period of one to three years has passed. This is to allow other organizations a chance to get funded.

Most governmental agencies do not impose any type of limitation on resubmissions. I would definitely advise grant writers to resubmit their application (with any updates) several times. One of my clients received funding for a water system rehabilitation on the third try. In this case, it appeared that, in the first two rounds, other projects that were funded met what was considered to be a greater need. Fortunately, on the third round, the other projects did not appear as worthy as this one. It just depends on the strength of the other applications. The rule of thumb here is to reapply if, after talking to the funding agency, your project appears to be worthy and meets all of the basic threshold requirements.

WHEN YOU SHOULD FIND OTHER POTENTIAL SOURCES

In the chapter on strategy development (chapter 6), I stress the importance of applying to multiple sources of funds. I have found that it is not productive to put all of one's faith into one particular funding agency or foundation. The odds of getting funded are much greater if multiple sources are developed and applied to concurrently. Much valuable time can be wasted in "putting all your eggs in one basket." Many programs only invite applications once a year. If an applicant decides to stick with that particular source, it could be two or three years before funding is received, if at all. This would unnecessarily delay the good work that would be accomplished by the project.

I would therefore strongly advise the grant writer against waiting through several rounds of a competition for one particular funding agency before applying to another source. This would be my advice even if the first source was clearly the best bet. Most of the time, two or three funding programs can be identified to fund a particular project, with all of them being equally promising. I have seen any number of grant writers give up after one rejection. This may be tied to a belief that one source is the only possibility. It is necessary to maintain a "can-do" attitude. Very few of the projects with which I have been involved have failed completely to receive at least partial funding. Sometimes this has taken several years, but it is necessary to be persistent.

Appendix A

Glossary

Abstract: A concise, abbreviated description of the contents of a grant application. This summary will generally be no longer than one page. It is not required for every grant application.

ACH (Automated Clearing House): A form utilized by funding agencies to set up the transfer of funds to a grantee. This form contains information about the grantee's bank account that will allow the agency to make direct deposits.

Assurances and Certifications: A list of applicable laws, regulations, and policies that the grantee will be expected to follow if funds are awarded. This document is typically signed at the time of application submittal.

Beneficiaries: The group(s) benefiting from a particular program.

Best Practices: Methodology and program procedures that have been shown to be the most effective in a particular field and that can be duplicated elsewhere.

Block Grants: Funds allocated to a state or a municipality for a broad range of purposes. The grantee will have varying degrees of discretion as to how these funds are used depending upon the program from which they have been awarded.

Budget Modification: A change in the original budget for a project. This can be originated by either the funding agency or the grantee. Many agencies require that this request, if coming from the grantee, be submitted on a standard form.

Budget Narrative: A brief narrative summary explaining the various budget items. For example, a budget for overtime would require a narrative that discusses the number of hours to be worked, the hourly overtime rate, and the projects that the overtime will address.

Capital Grants: Grants made for land acquisition, building construction, building renovation, or major pieces of equipment.

Catalog of Federal Domestic Assistance (CFDA): A document published by the federal government that lists all past and current federal grant opportunities. There is a brief description of program requirements and each grant is assigned a number. The CFDA can be accessed at http://www.cfda.gov.

Central Contractor Registry (CCR): A Web site maintained by the federal government that contains profiles of various governmental entities, nonprofits, and for-profit businesses. This profile contains information concerning the operations of those registered. It is necessary to have a registration in CCR in order to utilize Grants.gov. CCR can be accessed at http://www.ccr.gov.

Clearinghouse: The state agency assigned to review all requests for federal assistance in order to determine whether they are consistent with the policies, plans, and programs of the applicable agencies in that particular state. This requirement was mandated by Executive Order 12372, but does not apply to each state. The applicant is responsible for sending summaries of the application to the agency designated as the "Clearinghouse." The clearinghouse then distributes the proposal to various state agencies for their review. Any inconsistencies are noted in a letter to the applicant along with a recommended corrective plan of action in order to bring the project into consistency.

Collaboration: Two or more grantee organizations working together to implement a project.

Community Foundation: A grant-making foundation that usually serves a local area, often no more than three or four counties. Its funds are usually derived from families and individuals who wish to see their money go to projects undertaking specific types of activities and program areas.

Corporate Giving: Programs developed by private firms, usually medium to large corporations. These programs are often geared to specific interests of the corporation and are usually limited to geographic areas in which the firm has a presence.

Data Universal Numbering System (DUNS): A system of registration of various business, nonprofit, and governmental entities operated by the firm of Dun and Bradstreet. This system assigns a unique nine-digit identifying number to registrants and provides detailed information on the registrant's operations. Any applicant for federal financial assistance must obtain a DUNS number and provide it on the SF424. To find out more, go to http://www.dnb.com.

Demographics: Statistical data regarding a particular geographic area or service population. This is usually derived from the most recent Census and can include such information as total population, ethnicity, household income, age, gender, handicap status, housing characteristics, and level of education attained.

Discretionary Grants: Funding available under a competitive grant process, usually in a situation in which specific rating and ranking factors are taken into account in order to arrive at a total score that is compared against that of other applicants. The opposite of discretionary grants are entitlement grants.

Drawdowns: Requests for payment by the funding agency to the grantee once funds are awarded. There is usually a specific form that must be used. It is at the discretion of the funding agency as to whether documentation of costs must be submitted with the drawdown request.

Employer Identification Number (EIN): This number is assigned to businesses, nonprofits, and governmental entities by the Internal Revenue Service. Nearly every governmental grant program requires that this number be provided on the application.

Entitlement Grants: Funding that is provided on a formula basis, without competition; however, these programs require the submission of some type of application.

Environmental Review: All federal grants and federal money being passed through the states to localities require that certain documents be completed that specify the impact of the projects funded by these grant dollars upon the environment. This requirement was mandated by the National Environmental Policy Act. Part of the process involves informing the public of the findings.

Evaluation Plan: A standard requirement of many governmental and foundation grants that requests the applicant to specify how it will measure the success of the project.

Federal Register: A publication of the U.S. Government Printing Office that gives information on grant solicitations, requests for comment on federal government rules and regulations, and the final version of those rules and regulations. This publication is available both in paper form and online.

Goals and Objectives: A goal is a major, overriding, desired result for a particular project. Objectives are specific measurable results that will further the achievement of the goal.

Grant Agreement: A document generated by the agency or foundation awarding grant funds that spells out the terms and conditions of the grant award. The agreement is signed by both the funding agency and the grantee.

Grants.gov: An online grant research and submittal tool that is operated by the U.S. Department of Health and Human Services. It contains a description of every federal grant opportunity that is currently available from the participating agencies. Registration is required to utilize this tool to submit a grant application. Research into available grants does not require registration.

Income Survey: Required for some grant opportunities in which an area-wide benefit will result. The grantee must establish the fact that the area in question contains the required percentage/number of people in the low- and moderate-income category. The specific percentage of persons required being in this category and the income levels used to establish eligibility vary from program to program. Residents are generally required to fill out a survey form specifying the number of persons in the household and choosing from among several income categories without having to disclose their name or exact income.

Indirect Costs: Expenses associated with the general operation of an agency such as office rent, electricity, heating, and telephone costs. These costs cannot be directly attributable to a project per se.

In-Kind Contribution: Noncash resources committed to a project. This may include donations of materials and supplies as well as volunteer time and reductions in fees by professionals.

Inquiry Letter: A brief (two to three pages) letter that is primarily sent to private foundations as a way of determining whether there is any interest in the project. Many foundations require that the letter be sent as a first step prior to submitting a full application. This enables them to briefly assess whether a particular project meets their funding guidelines and criteria without having to read through the much longer application. Generally, this type of letter contains a brief description of the project, the organizational history, the capability of the applicant, the amount of funds requested, and expected outcomes.

Letter of Intent: A brief letter that is sent to a funding agency prior to the submittal of a full application in order to establish the applicant's interest. This is generally applicable mostly to government programs and is only required for certain solicitations.

Letter of Support: A letter from other organizations expressing their support for an applicant's project. Some programs require that letters of support be included with the application. However, these letters are generally optional.

Matching Funds: Funds dedicated to a project that come from sources other than the agency or foundation from whom funding is sought. Some grant programs require that the applicant provide some of the project costs. This has been the trend in the past several years, although many of the "stimulus" grant programs I have seen do not require a local match. The match generally ranges anywhere from 50 percent to 5 percent. In most cases, the government funding agencies and foundations require that the match be provided in cash.

Memorandum of Understanding: A document that details the various responsibilities and privileges pertaining to each party in a project that will be operated by more than one entity.

Monitoring Visit: A visit made by the funding agency to the grantee's offices in order to review the files concerning the project funded by a particular grant. This visit is made in order to establish whether the project was administered properly and in accordance with the applicable rules and regulations.

Notice of Funding Availability (NOFA): A notification from a funding agency to the public that it is accepting grant applications for a particular funding program.

Operating Grants: Grant funding that is utilized to support the costs of the general operations of an agency. This includes salaries, supplies, and equipment.

Organizational Capacity: The ability of a particular organization to carry out its basic mission. Resources that are dedicated to enhance organizational capacity include additional cash, training, and skilled staff.

Pilot Program: A program that is being initiated on an experimental basis in order to determine the impact of a permanent or longer-term project.

Preapplication: Some federal and state programs require that an applicant submit a preapplication prior to submitting a full application. In my experience, the preapplication is not, as one might expect, a short version of the application. In many cases, there is as much work involved in preparing a preapplication as there is in an application.

Private Operating Foundation: A designation given by the Internal Revenue Service to organizations that carry out their own charitable services, including research and direct assistance to individuals or disadvantaged groups. Private operating foundations do not generally give grants on a competitive basis.

Program Grants: Assistance given to organizations to carry out specific activities such as a lecture series, job training assistance, or a feeding program for the homeless.

Project Period: The length of time given to a grantee to complete the project.

Public Charity: A designation assigned by the Internal Revenue Service to an organization that raises the bulk of its funds from the general public.

Rating and Ranking Criteria: Factors used by an agency to determine the number of points assigned to a particular application. When utilizing this method, funding agencies will generally award grants to those applicants having the greatest number of points until the available funds are exhausted. These criteria are, in many cases, dictated by the regulations governing a particular program.

Scope of Work: A description of the tasks involved in successfully carrying out a particular project.

Seed Grant: Funds given to help an organization get started or to initiate a particular program within an existing organization.

Site Visit: A visit made by the staff of a funding agency to the site of a project proposed for funding. The purpose of the visit is to fill in any missing data, to receive the benefits of actually seeing a site or project as opposed to reading about it, to meet key staff to get an idea of their capability, and to meet prospective beneficiaries in order to get a clearer picture of the need for the project.

Standard Form 424: This multipage form is required for all federal applications. It consists of a cover sheet, a budget form, and a list of assurances that the grantee must agree to by signing the form.

State Historic Preservation Officer (SHPO): The individual designated by each state's historic preservation agency to review requests for federal funding within that state. The purpose of this review is to ascertain whether the proposed project will have an adverse impact upon historic resources.

Sustainability: The ability of the applicant to carry out the project once the grant has been expended. A project may be sustained by seeking other grants, using the organization's own budgeted funds, charging a service fee, or utilizing in-kind services.

Technical Assistance: Advice given by a funding agency to a grantee either in the application development stage or the post-approval phase.

Threshold Review: The initial review of an application by the funding agency. This will generally cover basic eligibility criteria without doing a complete rating and ranking. Agency staff will check to see that the applicant is an eligible applicant, that the project activity is an eligible activity, that the amount of the request is within the limits specified by the funding agency, and that various other criteria are met that establish the eligibility of the project, rather than its merits.

Timeline: The schedule by which the various components of the project will be undertaken. Nearly all funding agencies will request this information as part of the application.

Unrestricted funds: Donations made to an organization that may be used for any purpose.

Appendix B

Do's and Don'ts from the Funding Agencies

It is almost impossible to be successful in grant writing unless one is very much attuned to the thoughts of those reviewing the application. During the early part of my career, I was naturally somewhat hesitant and shy about approaching federal, state, and private officials about what to do and what not to do. However, I gained confidence as I went along and began to see that most staff members at the funding agencies actually welcome the opportunity to provide feedback to applicants. Before long, I was having direct and to-the-point conversation with these officials on almost a daily basis. My clients deserve to have the best product possible. If something needs clarification, it is my responsibility to get it.

My relationship with reviewing officials has made my job much easier. We freely share ideas back and forth. This has provided invaluable information that has greatly helped me in the quest for grant funds. The following is a compendium of what I have heard them say over the years. Much of this will seem like common sense, but it bears repeating. I have seen enough applications where directions have not been followed, the formatting is not done properly, or avoidable mistakes have been made. This list provides a quick and easy way of digesting the body of knowledge I have obtained over the years from those who have control over the money. If the grant writer follows these rules and works diligently at grant searches and on the grant applications, she can count on an impressive level of success. Following this list, I have detailed an interview I conducted with Dr. Spicer Bell, E.D.D., Executive Director of the Community Foundation of the Eastern Shore (CFES) of Salisbury, Maryland; and Ms. Erica Joseph, Program Director at CFES. Both Bell and Joseph were kind enough to provide me with valuable advice.

DO . . .

In General:

- Read through the entire NOFA before starting the application.
- Review the NOFA with an eye toward looking for deal breakers.
- Identify the need before proposing a solution or searching for funds, and quantify the extent of the need.
- Gather as much statistical and background data as possible before designing the project.

Designing the Project:

- Discuss possible solutions with key people prior to designing the project—get as much input as possible.
- Discuss the project with funding agency staff by telephone or e-mail before starting the application.
- Review the solutions implemented by other organizations that have a similar need—however, be aware of your unique circumstances.
- If necessary, be willing to travel to see other projects that have a bearing on yours. If this is not possible, talk on the telephone.
- Think "outside of the box" when developing a project—the sky is the limit!
- Use common sense in project development—sometimes your own best judgment is the answer!

Search:

- Look for organizations in the area that offer the free use of search resources, including *Foundation Center Online*. This could include community foundations, colleges, and universities.
- Call a potential funding source if there is some doubt as to whether it should be included in your search results. When making these calls, go to the trouble of finding out which staff member can best help.
- Check several grant search resources—try at least three or four.
- When doing a search, do not hesitate to contact peers in other organizations for ideas.
- When writing the results of a grant search, develop a clear strategy for action that is realistic and offers the best chance of receiving funding as soon as possible.
- Follow up on letters of inquiry to foundations if no response is received. Many foundations do not reply.

Application Process:

- Make letters of inquiry brief (no more than two pages) but informative—stress the need for the project, your organization's ability to carry it out, and the benefits that will accrue from it.
- Respond promptly if a foundation requests a full proposal based on a letter of inquiry.
- Check the Web site of a funding agency thoroughly before e-mailing or telephoning so as to avoid asking questions that are clearly answered on the Web site.
- Ensure that you have the latest version of the application and regulations.
- Check the math in the budget—although this is obvious, many applicants make mathematical errors.
- Pay attention to those agencies that require that a Letter of Intent be filed prior to a full application. In nearly all cases, there is a specific deadline for submitting this letter.
- Pay careful attention to the rating and ranking criteria when crafting a proposal. Incorporate the application language into the narrative.
- Be concise but thorough in the narrative.
- If there is a specific page maximum, be sure that you come as close to that as possible without exceeding it. You can rest assured that the other applicants will provide as much information as possible.
- Give a descriptive narrative with specific examples.
- Be crystal clear in your writing. Do not "beat around the bush."
- Be complete and thorough in the narrative—do not leave the reviewer wondering what you mean. Answer the questions completely.
- Use correct grammar, punctuation, and spelling.
- Reread the application at least twice.
- Give proper attribution for all information derived from others, and cite sources for statistical data.
- Answer the funding agency's requests for additional information completely, cheerfully, and on time.
- Send letters of support with the application itself unless the guidelines state otherwise. However, some U.S. Representatives and Senators will only send support letters directly to the funding agency.
- If there is any doubt whatsoever about whether an application will reach the office of the funding agency on time, send it overnight or two-day guaranteed delivery.
- Send the application directly to the person named in the solicitation, with the correct number of copies.
- Check to see that the application arrived on time.
- Start online applications early so that you can get your questions answered before the deadline.

- Keep the username and password for online applications in a handy place where they will not be lost.
- Do your best to stave off performance anxiety as the due date for the application arrives—this will impair your ability to do the best job possible.
- Do your best to be available for site visits when the funding agency wants to come. Only change the date if there is an emergency.

Project Administration:

- Sign and return the grant acceptance documents promptly.
- Read the grant agreement carefully.
- Call the funding agency or foundation with any questions regarding the administration of the funds. They would rather have you call frequently than have a mess to clean up at the time of the audit. They are worried about those grantees who do not call.
- Ensure as much accuracy in financial recordkeeping as humanly possible. This is what the funding agencies will check first.
- Begin to implement your project as soon as you possibly can. Funding agencies do not like to give extensions and, in many cases, will not give them for any reason.
- If you are passing funds through to a subrecipient, monitor their work closely. Your agency will be held accountable if anything goes wrong.
- Check to see what procurement procedures the funding agency requires for any purchases.
- Check periodically during implementation to be sure that the project is meeting the need and fulfilling the goals.
- For projects involving individual beneficiaries, be sure to get all of the pertinent information qualifying that individual or family (such as income verification) prior to approving or disbursing any benefits.
- Be completely cooperative during a monitoring visit, and provide everything the funding agency asks for.
- Answer any monitoring findings completely and promptly. Funding for your next project will depend upon it!
- Keep accurate and up-to-date records as the project proceeds.

DON'T . . .

Project Design:

- Be in a hurry to design a project and make mistakes just to meet a deadline—this wastes precious time.

Search:

- Count on one source of funding—have several in mind if possible.
- Feel as if you are "bothering" a potential funding source when calling to see if they are a possibility. It is their job to respond to you.
- Rely on what other applicants for the same funding are telling you—check it out for yourself.
- Rush through a grant search—this is one area where it pays to invest the extra time.
- Include in your grant search results a foundation that appears to have a very narrowly focused intent, one not accepting applications, or one that contributes only to preselected organizations. The foundations are very firm about this.
- Become discouraged when trying to discern whether a potential source is a good match. This often takes a significant amount of experience and in many cases is an "art," rather than a "science."
- Develop a grant-seeking strategy that is overly ambitious—be realistic about staff capacity.

Application Process:

- Ignore a funding agency's request for additional information.
- Intentionally deceive a funding agency.
- Maintain an overly optimistic attitude about receiving funding when a particular program is highly competitive—be realistic.
- Be afraid to apply to multiple sources at one time. This strategy offers the best chance of success. Funding agencies like to know that applicants are not depending solely on them.
- Be afraid to seek clarification on the application requirements.
- Rearrange the order of the questions in an application. Answer them in the exact order they are in the application, and repeat the question itself in the narrative.
- Avoid answering certain questions in the application due to insufficient information or because an answer might "make me look bad." Review panels will spot this immediately and will think that you either have something to hide or you do not have the pertinent information.
- Make sustainability promises that cannot be kept. However, be optimistic and, if no other prospects for continuation appear reasonable, say that you will look for other grants.
- Over-dramatize the scope of the need—state it just as it is, but be sure to bring out all of the negative consequences that will occur if the need is not addressed.

- Develop an evaluation plan that is unrealistic or that is beyond the capabilities of staff and consulting resources. Once you state how you will evaluate a project, you must stick to it.
- Add unnecessary appendices to the application. Add only what is directly relevant. Do not use the appendices section to add to the length of the narrative.
- Feel that you must deliver the application in person.
- Assume anything—always check the facts!
- Call the funding agency or foundation asking for a decision less than 45 days from the time the application was submitted.

Project Administration:

- Exaggerate progress achieved when writing reports.
- Pay contractors before getting any required information or reports.

Bell and Joseph substantially echoed the points that have been made above. The reason for this, of course, is that there seem to be certain universal rules in this profession that can make or break a request for funds. Bell stressed the importance of talking to funding officials prior to submitting an application. He feels that this is also a good way to develop contacts that will help future efforts. If the official that the grant writer reaches is not the correct one to contact, ask him to suggest someone else who is knowledgeable. However, Joseph made the additional comment that calling at the last minute does not make a good impression. It is therefore advisable to make these contacts during the planning stages of writing the grant application.

Joseph also stressed the importance of effective research and planning prior to beginning the application. She cautioned the grant writer against submitting full proposals to a foundation without checking to see whether either the applicant or the project is even eligible. A good part of the grant writer's skill consists of using resources in a wise fashion. Unfortunately, she is aware that many grant writers do not even do the basics in checking a potential source.

Bell stated that it is much better to be upfront and honest with funding agencies from the very beginning. He emphasized that "they just want to know the truth" so that they formulate the correct strategy for how to approach the situation. This makes everyone's job much easier. In addition, he stated that it is important for the grantee organization to produce the results promised in the application. Simply put, he advises to "do what you say you are going to do." Joseph concurred, saying that it is much better to tell the truth, even if it is unflattering, than to have to explain later why an inaccurate picture was painted.

In regard to the narrative section of the application, Bell stressed the importance of being brief and to the point in a tightly written, focused narrative.

An application written in this fashion will be much easier for the reviewers to understand. The natural tendency is to assign higher points for something that is simple to follow. He feels that wordy and extraneous material detracts from the story the grant writer is trying to tell. Both governmental and private grant reviewers see the inclusion of this additional material as a lack of professionalism and lack of knowledge about what the program is trying to accomplish. Joseph recommended that the grant writer have someone else in her organization read the application prior to submission in order to make sure that the story is told in an understandable fashion. She suggested that the applicant agency write the grant application so that a lay person would be able to understand it. All outcomes should be conveyed very clearly, as this is one of the most important parts of the application. All sections of the application should tie in together to make a cohesive story.

Both Bell and Joseph expressed the opinion that the grant writer could benefit from taking a class in general writing skills. Bell stated that the best writing comes as a result of good coaching and that there is no substitute for this type of mentoring. Both agree there are numerous resources available to teach both general writing and grant writing. The art and science of grant writing, according to them, can be mastered with sufficient time and attention.

Appendix C

Common Federal Grant Forms

**Sample CDBG Application—Washington State;
June 2009 Solicitation**

CDBG-PROJECT SUMMARY				
1. Grant Type:	X CDBG			
2. **Jurisdiction:**		Phone:		
Address—Mail:		Fax:		
Address—Street:		Fed Tax ID:		
City, Zip:		County:		
Email:		SWV Number:		
		DUNS Number:		
3. **Contact Person:**		Title:		
Address—Mail:		Phone:		
Address—Street:		Fax:		
City, Zip:				
Email:				
4. **Subrecipient:**		Title:		
Contact Person:		Phone:		
Address—Mail:		Fax:		
Address—Street:		Organization		
City, Zip:		Category(s):		
Email:		DUNS Number:		

5. **Consultant:**		Phone	
Address:		Fax:	
City, Zip:		Email:	

6. Fiscal Year:	From:	To:

7. State Legislative District: Congressional District:

8. Brief Project Description:

9. Did a CDBG Planning-Only Grant lead to this application?   ❐ Yes   ❐ No

10. Project Budget:	CDBG-R	$	
	Other Federal Recovery	$	
	Other Federal (non-Recovery)	$	*State funds may include Housing Trust Fund, Captial Funds or Public Works Board.
	State*	$	
	Local Public	$	
	Private	$	
	TOTAL	$	

11. Project Beneficiaries:	# of Persons		LMI Percentage:
	# of LMI Persons:		____ %
	# of Households		CDBG-R Investment per Household:
	# of LMI Households		$____

12. How were the beneficiaries determined?	❐ HUD's 2000 Census LMI List
For Limited Clientele, Housing, or Economic Development Jobs activities, check the "Direct Benefit Only" box.	❐ HUD's 2000 Census LMI Block Group Data
	❐ Income Survey /Date:
	❐ Direct Benefit Only

13. Certification of Chief Administrative Official:

The investment of American Recovery and Reinvestment Act funds for this project is an appropriate use of taxpayer dollars and I commit to adhere to the laws and regulations governing the Community Development Block Grant—Recovery Grant program.

_____   _____

Signature   Date

_____   _____

Print Name   Title

CITIZEN PARTICIPATION/PROJECT PRIORITIZATION CHECKLIST

HUD has waived the public hearing requirement for CDBG-R applications. However, a local government must document how its residents had access to information and the opportunity to participate in a local process for prioritizing needs and identifying projects for public funding.

√   Check which of the following opportunities were offered within the last 18 months (since October 2007) that apply to this application's project and the most recent occurrence:

❐   The need for the project was discussed at an open city/town council or county board meeting.
Most recent date:

❐   The need for the project was stated at a local public hearing
Most recent date:

❐   The project was identified as a priority by a public input process, such as a needs survey or community forum.
Most recent date:

❐   Other

√   Check which of your local government plans identifies this application's project, or the need to be addressed by this application, as a priority:

❐   Comprehensive land use plan
❐   Economic development plan
❐   Capital facilities plan
❐   Water, sewer, street or other system plan
❐   Community strategic plan
❐   Other (please specify)

If funded, CTED will require documentation of the "checked" citizen participation and project prioritization activities.

EVALUATION CRITERIA

1. Impact to community and benefit to LMI persons
2. Jobs created
3. Energy efficiency
4. Readiness to proceed
5. Funds leveraged and committed

EVALUATION QUESTIONS

What is the proposed project?

1. How would CDBG-R funding of this project impact the community at large and lower income persons specifically, both in the short- and long-term?

2. Approximately how many direct FTE jobs will this project create or retain? Explain your method for estimating the number. (See Job Creation Estimates page for more guidance.)

Type of Job	Permanent (including microenterprise jobs)	Construction	Other (explain)
Number FTE			

Job estimation method:

3. How will this project improve energy efficiency? Provide an approximate annual measure of the type of energy directly saved. (See Energy Efficiency Projects page for more information.)

4. Explain how this project is ready to proceed.

5. Complete the attached Work Plan. Priority will be given to:
   - ❏ Construction projects able to award bids by October 1, 2009
   - ❏ Microenterprise loan programs offering loan services by October 1, 2009

WORK PLAN

For projects that will not have NEPA/SEPA environmental review complete and will not be ready to award bids this fall, we recommend **not** applying for a CDBG Recovery Grant and instead applying for a CDBG General Purpose Grant this fall.

❏ *List the local responsible party and when you expect activities to be completed (month/year).*
❏ *Use the "Other" lines or insert lines for additional project tasks applicable to your project.*
❏ *Construction activities are highlighted and would not be applicable for microenterprise loan programs.*
❏ *See line-by-line instructions on the back.*

Task	Responsible Party	Start Date	End Date
Execute Grant Agreement with CTED		7/09	8/09
Establish Subrecipient Agreement, if applicable			
Establish local grant/loan program procedures and materials, if applicable			
Procure Professional Services			
Obtain Site Control			
Complete Cultural/Historical Resources Review			
Complete NEPA/SEPA Environmental Review			
Obtain Permits			
Prepare Bid Documents/Solicit Bids			
Award Construction Contract			
Start Construction			
Submit First Week Labor Standards Package			
Recovery fund job creation and progress reporting		10/09 and Qrtly	
Complete Construction			
Other			
Other			
Other			
Conduct Final Public Hearing			
Project in Use—Building occupancy, utility in service, microenterprise loans closed, etc.			

PROJECT BUDGET

There are two budget components in this application:
1) Budget Assumptions (no format is provided with this application)
2) Project Budget Form

BUDGET ASSUMPTIONS INSTRUCTIONS

Tell us how you built the budget, explaining how you derived costs for each activity cost in your budget form. Your assumptions should include the following:

❑ Why is this budget reasonable and appropriate, considering the scope, substance, and duration of the proposed project?

❑ What are the assumptions behind the activity cost calculations? Be detailed and specific.

❑ Are you proposing to purchase equipment that would cost over $300? If yes, describe.

Attach available source documentation of the costs, such as an engineer's preliminary costs.

Add pages as needed to complete your assumptions.

PROJECT BUDGET					
Funding Status	Source 1	Source 2	Source 3	Source 4	
Are the sources committed?	CDBG-R	☐Yes ☐ No	☐Yes ☐ No	☐Yes ☐ No	**Totals**
Is it an ARRA recovery fund source?	☒Yes ☐ No	☐Yes ☐ No	☐Yes ☐ No	☐Yes ☐ No	
Activity Costs					
General Administration (CDBG-R contract execution, files and record keeping, civil rights compliance)					
Project Administration (Project Manager, Consultant Fees)					
Environmental Review					
Architectural Fees					
Engineering Fees					
Acquisition					
Relocation					
Sewer Improvements					
Water Improvements					
Water/Sewer Side Connections					
Street Improvements					
Community Facility					
Fire Protection Facility					
Housing Rehabilitation					
Architectural Barrier Removal					
ED Revolving Loan Fund Program					
Commercial/Industrial Facility					
Other:					
Other:					
Totals					

Use a second copy of this form if you have more than 4 funding sources

WASHINGTON (D.C.)

Regional Association of

GRANT MAKERS
Common Grant Application

Formatting notes

- Proposals should be printed on white paper, using a 12-point font (Times or similar) and one-inch margins on all sides; pages should be numbered.
- Proposals should not be placed in binders or folders; one staple or paper clip in the upper-left hand corner, securing all pages, is sufficient.

I. Executive Summary (1–2 pages, single-spaced)

1. Application date
2. Organization's name and contact information (full address, including mailing address if different, telephone, fax, and Web address)
3. Organization's federal tax-exempt number
4. Contact person's name, title, and contact information (telephone, fax, e-mail)
5. Dollar amount of this funding request
6. Total program budget (if applicable)
7. Total current organizational budget and fiscal year
8. Period this funding request will cover
9. Purpose of this funding request, including target population, number of individuals, and geographic area(s) that will benefit from this proposal
10. Brief organizational history and brief description of previous year's accomplishments
11. Total support from this funder for the past three years: List year, amount, and purpose for all support
12. Signature of executive director

II. Narrative (No more than 8 double-spaced pages)

1. **For All Requests:** Information on Your Organization
    1. Describe, in one paragraph, the organization's history, mission, and goals.
    2. Describe current programs and activities, and recent organizational accomplishments.

3. How will this request enable the organization to build its capacity, address current limitations, and/or improve its ability to meet program or organizational goals?

4. Describe briefly the involvement of your target population(s) in implementing the work of the organization, if applicable.

PLEASE COMPLETE THE ONE SECTION BELOW WHICH IS RELEVANT TO THIS REQUEST. Be sure that the foundation to which you are applying supports the type of request you are making.

B. For Program Requests (including capacity building projects)

1. What is the issue/need to be addressed and evidence of that need?

2. For a **new** program: how was the program approach developed?

3. For an **ongoing** program: what measurable *outcomes (defined as concrete changes or impact)* have been achieved over the past year?

4. Does this program use best practices—i.e., is this program based on a program that has been shown to be effective in other settings, based on national standards, etc? If so, please describe.

5. What is the plan for implementation? (Narrative, table, or logic model format is acceptable.) What existing community resources (e.g., facilities, people) will be used? If applicable: what is the target population's involvement in *this program's* development and implementation?

6. Based on the implementation plan, what measurable outcomes will be achieved during this grant period? What are the measurable longer-term outcomes of this program? What methods/strategies will be used to gather data on the project? How will the program evaluation be used?

7. How does this program fit into the work of this organization?

8. How does this program relate to the work of other organizations in the same field and/or geographic area?

9. What resources (financial, personnel, partnerships, etc.) will be needed to sustain this effort over time? How will those resources be secured?

C. For General Support Requests

1. What are the issue(s) or need(s) to be addressed and the evidence of those issues or needs?

2. For a **new** organization: how and why was the organization formed?

3. For an **existing** organization: what measurable *outcomes (defined as concrete change or impact)* have been achieved over the past year?

4. Does the organization use best practices—i.e., are any programs or operations based on ones that have been shown to be effective in other settings, based on national standards, etc? If so, please describe.

5. What are the plans for the organization's major program activities? (Narrative or table format is acceptable.) What existing community resources (e.g., facilities, people) will be used?

6. Based on these activities, what measurable outcomes will be achieved during this grant period? What are the measurable longer-term outcomes of the organization's work? What methods/strategies will be used to gather data? How will the evaluation be used?

7. How does the work of this organization relate to the work of other organizations in the same field and/or geographic area?

8. What resources (financial, personnel, partnerships, etc.) will be needed to sustain the organization over time? How will those resources be secured?

D. For Capital Campaign Requests: Capital campaign requests are designated for the acquisition, construction, renovation, or improvement of a property. Include information on the following, as applicable to your organization's request.

1. Discuss the need, feasibility, and cost of the capital campaign, and its implications for the organization's ongoing operational expenses.

2. Specify contributions in hand as well as pending or prospective.

3. Specify loans, including amounts and terms.

4. Include the financial participation in the campaign of the board and the capital/leadership campaign committee (percent participating and total contributed).

5. Specify whether purchase agreements or purchase options are signed or imminent. Specify also whether regulatory approvals (e.g., Certificate of Need, zoning, historic preservation, environmental impact) in place or are imminent.

6. Indicate if timing is a factor, i.e., if a "window of opportunity" exists that affects the success of the campaign.

III. Finances (for all requests)—This information is not considered part of the narrative.

The following information must accompany all proposals, regardless of the size of the request. Not all categories may be applicable to your organization or request. You may submit this information in the format most convenient to you; it must, however, include as much of the following detail as possible. Footnotes may be used to explain budget items.

A. For all requests

1. Fiscal year

2. Financial statements:
   a. For previous fiscal year: organizational budget v. actual, for both revenue and expenses (using categories below)

      b. For current fiscal year:
- i. Organizational budget v. actual, for both revenue and expenses (using categories below)
- ii. Organization's year-to-date Statement of Financial Position (Balance Sheet) and year-to-date Statement of Activities (Income Statement)

      c. If this application is being made during the last quarter of the organization's fiscal year, provide the organization's projected/proposed/draft budget for the next fiscal year

3. If available: most recent audited financial statements (include auditor's letter and notes). If you do not have an audit, provide pages 1–6 of most recent IRS Form-990.

B. **For Program Requests** (including capacity building and capital campaign requests)—In addition to the information requested above:

1. Financial statements:
   - a. For previous fiscal year: program budget v. actual, for both revenue and expenses (using categories below)
   - b. For current fiscal year: program budget v. actual, for both revenue and expenses (using categories below)
   - c. If this application is being made during the last quarter of the organization's fiscal year, provide the program's projected/proposed/draft budget for the next fiscal year

Revenue Categories: For each category, list specific amounts requested from foundations, corporations, and other funding sources for this proposal, as well as the status of those requests (pending or committed). For pending requests, please indicate the date you expect notification.

1. Grants/Contracts:
   - a. Local/State/Federal Governments (please list source(s))
   - b. Foundations
   - c. Corporations
   - d. United Way/Combined Federal Campaign and other federated campaigns
   - e. Individual donors
   - f. Other (specify)
2. Earned Revenue
   - a. Events
   - b. Publications and Products
   - c. Fees
   - d. Other (specify)
3. Membership Income
4. In-Kind Support (donated goods, services, equipment, non-cash items, volunteer hours)

5. Other (specify)
6. Total Revenue

Expense categories: Include the total amount for each category relevant to your organization. Skip categories where you have no expenses. Please show two columns—one listing the total expense and one listing the specific costs requested in this grant proposal.

1. Salaries (total salary budget, number of positions, and whether full- or part-time)
2. Payroll Taxes
3. Fringe Benefits
4. Consultants and Professional Fees (itemize type(s) of consultant(s) and fees)
5. Travel
6. Equipment
7. Supplies
8. Printing and Copying
9. Telephone and Fax
10. Postage and Delivery
11. Rent and Utilities
12. Maintenance
13. Technology (if budgeted separately—specify hardware/software capital spending, maintenance, and/or training)
14. Evaluation
15. In-kind expenses
16. Other (specify)
17. Total Expenses

IV. Required Attachments (for all requests)—This information is not considered part of the narrative.

A copy of your current IRS tax-exempt determination letter. If tax-exempt status is pending, provide an explanation of application status.

A one-page organizational chart.

Short biographies (no more than 1/2 page) of staff and volunteers essential to the success of this request.

List of board members with terms, occupations, and places of employment.

Current, dated Memoranda of Understanding or Memoranda of Agreement with other organizations for collaborative or cooperative activities, as appropriate.

For Capital Spending Projects: list of members of the capital campaign/leadership committee.

Annual report, if available.

OMB Number: 4040-0004
Expiration Date: 01/31/2009

Application for Federal Assistance Standard Form 424 (cover sheet)	Version 02

* 1. Type of Submission:
- ☐ Preapplication
- ☐ Application
- ☐ Changed/Corrected Application

* 2. Type of Application: *** If Revision, select appropriate letter(s):**
- ☐ New
- ☐ Continuation   *** Other (Specify)**
- ☐ Revision

* 3. Date Received:

Completed by Grants.gov upon submission.

4. Applicant Identifier:

5a. Federal Entity Identifier:

* 5b. Federal Award Identifier:

State Use Only:

6. Date Received by State:

7. State Application Identifier:

8. APPLICANT INFORMATION:

* a. Legal Name:

* b. Employer/Taxpayer Identification Number (EIN/TIN):

* c. Organizational DUNS:

d. Address:

* Street1:

Street2:

* City:

County:

* State:

Province:

* Country: USA: UNITED STATES

* Zip / Postal Code:

e. Organizational Unit:

Department Name:

Division Name:

OMB Number: 4040-0004
Expiration Date: 01/31/2009

Application for Federal Assistance
SF-424   Version 02

f. Name and contact information of person to be contacted on matters involving this application:

Prefix:		* First Name:	
Middle Name:			
* Last Name:			
Suffix:			

Title:

Organizational Affiliation:

* Telephone Number: Fax Number:

* Email:

9. Type of Applicant 1: Select Applicant Type:

Type of Applicant 2: Select Applicant Type:

Type of Applicant 3: Select Applicant Type:

* Other (specify):

* 10. Name of Federal Agency:

NGMS Agency

11. Catalog of Federal Domestic Assistance Number:

CFDA Title:

* 12. Funding Opportunity Number:

MBL-SF424FAMILY-ALLFORMS

* Title:

MBL-SF424Family-AllForms

OMB Number: 4040-0004
Expiration Date: 01/31/2009

Application for Federal Assistance
SF-424 Version 02

13. Competition Identification Number:

Title:

14. Areas Affected by Project (Cities, Counties, States, etc.):

* 15. Descriptive Title of Applicant's Project:

Attach supporting documents as specified in agency instructions.

Add Attachments   Delete Attachments   View Attachments

16. Congressional Districts Of:

* a. Applicant   * b. Program/Project

Attach an additional list of Program/Project Congressional Districts if needed.

Add Attachment   Delete Attachment   View Attachment

17. Proposed Project:

* a. Start Date: * b. End Date:

18. Estimated Funding ($):

* a. Federal

* b. Applicant

* c. State

* d. Local

* e. Other

OMB Number: 4040-0004
Expiration Date: 01/31/2009

Application for Federal Assistance
SF-424   Version 02

* f. Program Income	
*g. TOTAL	

* 19. Is Application Subject to Review By State Under Executive Order 12372 Process?

☐ a. This application was made available to the State under the Executive Order 12372 Process
for review on [   ] .

☐ b. Program is subject to E.O. 12372 but has not been selected by the State for review.

☐ c. Program is not covered by E.O. 12372.

* 20. Is the Applicant Delinquent On Any Federal Debt? (If "Yes", provide explanation.)

☐ Yes   ☐ No   [Explanation]

21. ***By signing this application, I certify (1) to the statements contained in the list of certifications** and (2) that the statements herein are true, complete and accurate to the best of my knowledge. I also provide the required assurances** and agree to comply with any resulting terms if I accept an award. I am aware that any false, fictitious, or fraudulent statements or claims may subject me to criminal, civil, or administrative penalties. (U.S. Code, Title 218, Section 1001)**

☐   **** I AGREE**

** The list of certifications and assurances, or an internet site where you may obtain this list, is contained in the announcement or agency specific instructions.

Authorized Representative:

Prefix:		* First Name:	
Middle Name:			
* Last Name:			
Suffix:			

* Title:	

* Telephone Number:		Fax Number:	

* Email:	

* Signature of Authorized Representative:	Completed by Grants.gov upon submission.	* Date Signed:	Completed by Grants.gov upon submission.

Authorized for Local Reproduction

Standard Form 424 (Revised 10/2005)
Prescribed by OMB Circular A-102

OMB Number: 4040-0004
Expiration Date: 01/31/2009

Application for Federal Assistance
SF-424   Version 02

* Applicant Federal Debt Delinquency Explanation

The following field should contain an explanation if the Applicant organization is delinquent on any Federal Debt. Maximum number of characters that can be entered is 4,000. Try and avoid extra spaces and carriage returns to maximize the availability of space.

OMB Approval No. 0348-0040

APPLICATION FOR FEDERAL ASSISTANCE
STANDARD FORM 424B

ASSURANCES—NON-CONSTRUCTION PROGRAMS

Public reporting burden for this collection of information is estimated to average 15 minutes per response, including time for reviewing instructions, searching existing data sources, gathering and maintaining the data needed, and completing and reviewing the collection of information. Send comments regarding the burden estimate or any other aspect of this collection of information, including suggestions for reducing this burden, to the Office of Management and Budget, Paperwork Reduction Project (0348-0040), Washington, DC 20503.

PLEASE DO NOT RETURN YOUR COMPLETED FORM TO THE OFFICE OF MANAGEMENT AND BUDGET. SEND IT TO THE ADDRESS PROVIDED BY THE SPONSORING AGENCY.

NOTE: Certain of these assurances may not be applicable to your project or program. If you have questions, please contact the awarding agency. Further, certain Federal awarding agencies may require applicants to certify to additional assurances. If such is the case, you will be notified.

As the duly authorized representative of the applicant, I certify that the applicant:

1. Has the legal authority to apply for Federal assistance and the institutional, managerial and financial capability (including funds sufficient to pay the non-Federal share of project cost) to ensure proper planning, management and completion of the project described in this application.

2. Will give the awarding agency, the Comptroller General of the United States and, if appropriate, the State, through any authorized representative, access to and the right to examine all records, books, papers, or documents related to the award; and will establish a proper accounting system in accordance with generally accepted accounting standards or agency directives.

3. Will establish safeguards to prohibit employees from using their positions for a purpose that constitutes or presents the appearance of personal or organizational conflict of interest, or personal gain.

4. Will initiate and complete the work within the applicable time frame after receipt of approval of the awarding agency.

5. Will comply with the Intergovernmental Personnel Act of 1970 (42 U.S.C. §§ 4728-4763) relating to prescribed standards for merit systems

for programs funded under of the 19 statutes or regulations specified in Appendix A of OPM's Standards for a Merit System of Personnel Administration (5 C.F.R. 900, Subpart F).

6. Will comply with all Federal statutes relating to nondiscrimination. These include but are not limited to; (a) Title VI of the Civil Rights Act of 1964 (P.L. 88-352) which prohibits discrimination on the basis of race, color or national origin; (b) Title IX of the Education Amendments of 1972, as amended (20 U.S.C. §§ 1681-1683, and 1685-1686), which prohibits discrimination on the basis of sex; (c) Section 504 of the Rehabilitation Act of 1973, as amended (29 U.S.C. § 794), which prohibits discrimination on the basis of handicaps; (d) the Age Discrimination Act of 1975, as amended (42 U.S.C. §§ 6101-6107), which prohibits discrimination on the basis of age; (e) the Drug Abuse Office and Treatment Act of 1972 (P.L. 92-255), as amended, relating to nondiscrimination on the basis of drug abuse; (f) the Comprehensive Alcohol Abuse and Alcoholism Prevention, Treatment and Rehabilitation Act of 1970 (P.L. 91-616), as amended, relating to nondiscrimination on the basis of alcohol abuse or alcoholism; (g) §§ 523 and 527 of the Public Health Service Act of 1912 (42 U.S.C. §§ 290 dd-3 and 290 ee 3), as amended, relating to confidentiality of alcohol and drug abuse patient records; (h) Title VIII of the Civil Rights Act of 1968 (42 U.S.C. §§ 3601 et seq.), as amended, relating to nondiscrimination in the sale, rental or financing of housing; (i) any other nondiscrimination provisions in the specific statute(s) under which application for Federal assistance is being made; and, (j) the requirements of any other nondiscrimination statute(s) which may apply to the application.

7. Will comply, or has already complied, with the requirements of Titles II and III of the Uniform Relocation Assistance and Real Property Acquisition one Policies Act of 1970 (P.L. 91-646) which provide for fair and equitable treatment of persons displaced or whose property is acquired as a result of Federal or federally-assisted programs. These requirements apply to all interests in real property acquired for project purposes regardless of Federal participation in purchases.

8. Will comply, as applicable, with provisions of the Hatch Act (5 U.S.C. §§ 1501-1508 and 7324-7328) which limit the political activities of employees whose principal employment activities are funded in whole or in part with Federal funds.

9. Will comply, as applicable, with the provisions of the Davis-Bacon Act (40 U.S.C. §§ 276a to 276a-7), the Copeland Act (40 U.S.C, § 276c and 18 U.S.C. § 874), and the Contract Work Hours and Safety Standards Act (40 U.S.C. §§ 327-333), regarding labor standards for federally-assisted construction subagreements.

10. Will comply, if applicable, with flood insurance purchase requirements of Section 102(a) of the Flood Disaster Protection Act of 1973 (P.L. 93-234) which requires recipients in a special flood hazard area to participate in the program and to purchase flood insurance if the total cost of insurable construction and acquisition is $10,000 or more.

11. Will comply with environmental standards which may be prescribed pursuant to the following: (a) institution of environmental quality control measures under the National Environmental Policy Act of 1969 (P.L. 91-190) and Executive Order (EO) 11514; (b) notification of violating facilities pursuant to EO 11738; (c) protection of wetlands pursuant to EO 11990; (d) evaluation of flood hazards in floodplains in accordance with EO 11988; (e) assurance of project consistency with the approved State management program developed under the Coastal Zone Management Act of 1972 (16 U.S.C. §§ 1451 et seq.); (f) conformity of Federal actions to State (Clean Air) Implementation Plans under Section 176(c) of the Clean Air Act of 1955, as amended (42 U.S.C. §§ 7401 et seq.); (g) protection of underground sources of drinking water under the Safe Drinking Water Act of 1974, as amended (P.L. 93-523); and, (h) protection of endangered species under the Endangered Species Act of 1973, as amended (P.L. 93-205).

12. Will comply with the Wild and Scenic Rivers Act of 1968 (16 U.S.C. §§ 1271 et seq.) related to protecting components or potential components of the national wild and scenic rivers system.

13. Will assist the awarding agency in assuring compliance with Section 106 of the National Historic Preservation Act of 1966, as amended (16 U.S.C. § 470), EO 11593 (identification and protection of historic properties), and the Archaeological and Historic Preservation Act of 1974 (16 U.S.C. §§ 469a-1 et seq.).

14. Will comply with P.L. 93-348 regarding the protection of human subjects involved in research, development, and related activities supported by this award of assistance.

15. Will comply with the Laboratory Animal Welfare Act of 1966 (P.L. 89-544, as amended, 7 U.S.C.

§§ 2131 et seq.) pertaining to the care, handling, and treatment of warm blooded animals held for research, teaching, or other activities supported by this award of assistance.

16. Will comply with the Lead-Based Paint Poisoning Prevention Act (42 U.S.C. §§ 4801 et seq.) which prohibits the use of lead-based paint in construction or rehabilitation of residence structures.

17. Will cause to be performed the required financial and compliance audits in accordance with the Single Audit Act Amendments of 1996 and OMB Circular No. A-133, "Audits of States, Local Governments, and Non-Profit Organizations."

18. Will comply with all applicable requirements of all other Federal laws, executive orders, regulations, and policies governing this program.

SIGNATURE OF AUTHORIZED CERTIFYING OFFICIAL	TITLE	
APPLICANT ORGANIZATION		DATE SUBMITTED

Standard Form 424B (Rev. 7-97) Back

USDA   *Position 3*   FORM APPROVED
Form RD 1940-20   OMB No. 0575-0094
(Rev.4-06)   **REQUEST FOR ENVIRONMENTAL INFORMATION**

Name of Project
Location

Item 1a. Has a Federal, State, or Local Environmental Impact Statement or Analysis been prepared for this project?
  ❐ Yes   ❐ No   ❐ Copy attached as EXHIBIT I-A.
1b. If "No," provide the information requested in Instructions as EXHIBIT I.

Item 2. The State Historic Preservation Officer (SHOP) has been provided a detailed project description and has been requested to submit comments to the appropriate Rural Development Office.   ❐ Yes   ❐ No   Date description submitted to SHPO _____

Item 3. Are any of the following land uses or environmental resources either to be affected by the proposal or located within or adjacent to the project site(s)? *(Check appropriate box for every item of the following checklist).*

	Yes	No	Unknown			Yes	No	Unknown
1. Industrial	❐	❐	❐	19. Dunes		❐	❐	❐
2. Commercial	❐	❐	❐	20. Estuary		❐	❐	❐
3. Residential	❐	❐	❐	21. Wetlands		❐	❐	❐
4. Agricultural	❐	❐	❐	22. Floodplain		❐	❐	❐
5. Grazing	❐	❐	❐	23. Wilderness		❐	❐	❐
				(designated or proposed				
6. Mining, Quarrying	❐	❐	❐	*under the Wilderness Act)*				
				24. Wild or Scenic River		❐	❐	❐
7. Forests	❐	❐	❐	*(proposed or designated under*				
				the Wild and Scenic Rivers Act)				
8. Recreational	❐	❐	❐					
				25. Historical, Archeological Sites		❐	❐	❐
9. Transportation	❐	❐	❐	*(Listed on the National Register of*				
				Historic Places or which may be				
10. Parks	❐	❐	❐	*eligible for listing)*				
11. Hospital	❐	❐	❐	26. Critical Habitats		❐	❐	❐
				(endangered/threatened species)				
12. Schools	❐	❐	❐	27. Wildlife		❐	❐	❐
13. Open spaces	❐	❐	❐	28. AirQuality		❐	❐	❐
14. Aquifer Recharge Area	❐	❐	❐	29. Solid Waste Management		❐	❐	❐
15. Steep Slopes	❐	❐	❐	30. Energy Supplies		❐	❐	❐
16. Wildlife Refuge	❐	❐	❐	31. Natural Landmark		❐	❐	❐
				(Listed on National Registry				
17. Shoreline	❐	❐	❐	*of NaturalLandmarks)*				
18. Beaches	❐	❐	❐	32. Coastal Barrier Resources System		❐	❐	❐

Item 4. Are any facilities under your ownership, lease, or supervision to be utilized in the accomplishment of this project, either listed or under consideration for listing on the Environmental Protection Agency's List of Violating Facilities?   ❐ Yes   ❐ No

_____   Signed:_____
         (Date)   *(Applicant)*

                                            _____
                                                      (Title)

STATUTORY CHECKLIST

24 CFR § 58.5 STATUTES, EXECUTIVE ORDERS & REGULATIONS

Grant Recipient: _____ Project Name: _____

Project Description (Include all actions which are either geographically or func-
tionally related):

_____

_____

Location: _____

This project is determined to be categorically excluded according to: [Cite
section(s)] _____

Compliance Factors:

Statutes, Executive Orders, and Regulations listed at 24 CFR § 58.5	N/A	Consultation, Review, Permits Required	Consistency Determination	Condition, Mitigation	**Compliance Documentation**
Historic Preservation [36 CFR Part 800]					
Floodplain Management [24 CFR 55, Executive Order 11988]					
Wetland Protection [Executive Order 11990]					
Coastal Zone Management Act [Sections 307(c), (d)]					

Compliance Factors:

Statutes, Executive Orders, and Regulations listed at 24 CFR § 58.5	N/A	Consultation, Review, Permits Required	Consistency Determination	Condition, Mitigation	**Compliance Documentation**
Safe Drinking Water Act (42 USC 201, 300(f) & 21 U.S.C.349)					
Sole Source Aquifers [40 CFR 149]					
Endangered Species Act [50 CFR 402]					
Wild and Scenic Rivers Act [Sections 7(b), and (c)]					
Clean Air Act [Sections 176(c), (d), and 40 CFR 6, 51, 93]					
Farmland Protection Policy Act [7 CFR 658]					
Environmental Justice [Executive Order 12898]					
HUD ENVIRONMENTAL STANDARDS					
Noise Abatement and Control [24 CFR 51B]					

Compliance Factors:

Statutes, Executive Orders, and Regulations listed at 24 CFR § 58.5	N/A	Consultation, Review, Permits Required	Consistency Determination	Condition, Mitigation	**Compliance Documentation**
Explosive and Flammable Operations [24 CFR 51C]					
Toxic Chemicals and Radioactive Materials [24 CFR 58.5(i)]					
Airport Clear Zones and Accident Potential Zones [24 CFR 51D]					

DETERMINATION:

( ) This project converts to Exempt, per Section 58.34(a)(l2), because it does not require any mitigation for compliance with any listed statutes or authorities, nor requires any formal permit or license (Status "A" has been determined in the status column for all authorities); Funds may be drawn down for this (now) EXEMPT project; OR

( ) This project cannot convert to Exempt because one or more statutes/authorities require consultation or mitigation. Complete consultation/mitigation requirements, publish NOI/RROF and obtain Authority to Use Grant Funds (HUD 7015.16) per Section 58.70 and 58.71 before drawing down funds; OR

( ) The unusual circumstances of this project may result in a significant environmental impact. This project requires preparation of an Environmental Assessment (EA). Prepare the EA according to 24 CFR Part 58 Subpart E.

PREPARER SIGNATURE: _____ DATE: _____

PREPARER NAME: _____

RESPONSIBLE ENTITY AGENCY

OFFICIAL SIGNATURE: _____

NAME, TITLE: _____

DATE: _____

ERR Document **12/04 HUD Region VI**

FY 2008 Grantee Handbook Exhibit A-5

Appendix D

Grants.gov Step-by-Step Registration Process

ORGANIZATION REGISTRATION CHECKLIST

The following checklist provides registration guidance for a company, academic or research institution, state, local or tribal government, not-for-profit, or other type of organization. The registration is a **one-time** process, which is **required** before representatives of an organization can submit grant application packages electronically through Grants.gov. The registration process can take **three to five business days or one to three weeks** depending on your organization and if all steps are met in a timely manner.

*Note: If you are an individual applying for a grant on your own behalf and not on behalf of a company, academic or research institution, state, local or tribal government, not-for-profit, or other type of organization, refer to the **Individual Registration:** http://www.grants.gov/applicants/individual_registration.isp. If you apply as an individual to a grant application package designated for organizations, your application will be rejected.*

STEPS TO COMPLETE TO REGISTER AN ORGANIZATION	COMPLETED?
STEP 1: OBTAIN DUNS NUMBER	
Has my organization identified its Data Universal Number System (DUNS) number? Ask the grant administrator, chief financial officer, or authorizing official of your organization to identify your DUNS number. If your organization does not know its DUNS number or needs to register for one, visit Dun & Bradstreet at http://fedgov.dnb.com/webform/displayHomePage.do.	O

STEPS TO COMPLETE TO REGISTER AN ORGANIZATION	COMPLETED?
PURPOSE OF THIS STEP: The federal government has adopted the use of DUNS numbers to track how federal grant money is allocated. DUNS numbers identify your organization. **HOW LONG SHOULD IT TAKE?** Same Day. You will receive DUNS number information online.	
STEP 2: REGISTER WITH CCR	
Has my organization registered with the Central Contractor Registration (CCR)? Ask the grant administrator, chief financial officer, or authorizing official of your organization if your organization has registered with the CCR. If your organization is not registered, you can apply by phone (1-888-227-2423) or register online at http://www.ccr.gov. CCR has developed a handbook (http://www.ccr.gov/handbook.asp) to help you with the process. When your organization registers with CCR, you must designate an E-Business Point of Contact (E-Biz POC). This person will identify a special password called an "M-PIN." This M-PIN gives the E-Biz POC authority to designate which staff member(s) from your organization are allowed to submit applications electronically through Grants.gov. Staff members from your organization designated to submit applications are called Authorized Organization Representatives (AORs). **PURPOSE OF THIS STEP:** Registering with the CCR is required for organizations to use Grants.gov. **HOW LONG SHOULD IT TAKE?** If your organization already has an Employment Identification Number (EIN) or Taxpayer Identification Number (TIN), then you should allow one–three business days to complete the entire CCR registration. The EIN and TIN will come from the Internal Revenue Service (IRS) If your organization does not have an EIN or TIN, then you should allow two weeks for obtaining the information from the IRS when requesting the EIN or TIN via phone or Internet. The additional number of days needed is a result of security information that needs to be mailed to the organization.	O

*Note: *Your organization needs to renew their CCR registration once a year. You will not be able to move on to Step 3 until this step is completed. This step may take up to 5 business days.*

STEPS TO COMPLETE TO REGISTER AN ORGANIZATION	COMPLETED?
STEP 3: USERNAME & PASSWORD	
Have the AORs who officially submit applications on behalf of your organization completed their profile with Grants.gov to create their username and password? To create a username and password, AORs must complete their profile on Grants.gov. AORs will need to know the DUNS number of the organization for which they will be submitting applications to complete the process. After your organization registers with the CCR, AORs must wait one business day before they can complete a profile and create their usernames and passwords on Grants.gov. **PURPOSE OF THIS STEP:** An AOR username and password serves as an "electronic signature" when submitting a Grants.gov application. **HOW LONG SHOULD IT TAKE?** Same Day. After the AOR has completed their profile they will be prompted to create a username and password that will allow the user to login and check their approval status immediately.	O
STEP 4: AOR AUTHORIZATION	
Has the E-Business Point of Contact (E-Biz POC) approved AORs to submit applications on behalf of the organization? When an AOR registers with Grants.gov to submit applications on behalf of an organization, that organization's E-Biz POC will receive an email notification. The email the AOR submitted in the profile will be the email used when sending the automatic notification from Grants.gov to the E-Biz POC with the AOR copied on the correspondence. The E-Biz POC must then login to Grants.gov (using the organization's DUNS number for the username and the "M-PIN" password obtained in Step 2) and approve the AOR, thereby giving him or her permission to submit applications. When an E-Biz POC approves an AOR, Grants.gov will send the AOR a confirmation email. **PURPOSE OF THIS STEP:** Only the E-Biz POC can approve AORs. This allows the organization to authorize specific staff members or consultants/grant writers to submit grants. Only those who have been authorized by the E-Biz POC can submit applications on behalf of the organization. **HOW LONG SHOULD IT TAKE?** This depends on how long it takes the E-Biz POC to login and approve the AOR, once the approval is completed the AOR can immediately submit an application.	O

STEPS TO COMPLETE TO REGISTER AN ORGANIZATION	COMPLETED?
STEP 5: TRACK AOR STATUS	
AORs can also <u>login</u> to track their AOR status using their user-name and password (obtained in Step 3) to check if they have been approved by the E-Biz POC. **PURPOSE OF THIS STEP:** To verify that the organization's E-Biz POC has approved the AOR. **HOW LONG SHOULD IT TAKE?** Logging in as an applicant is instantaneous, the approval process to become an AOR depends on how long it takes the E-Biz POC to login and approve the AOR.	⭕

Appendix E

Sample Letter of Inquiry

(Date)

(Name and address of potential funder)

Ladies and Gentlemen:

A compelling opportunity has come our way to preserve one of the most notable historic properties on the Palmer Peninsula and thereby bring to the community a remarkable story of early plantation life along the coast. We are asking for support from federal, state, local, and private sources and hereby request a $25,000 grant from your foundation.

This is in reference to the Sherwood Plantation House located within the Coastal State Park. Sherwood House Trust, a nonprofit foundation, has been formed to lease the property from the state. Our mission is to restore the deteriorated structure to its stately 18th-century appearance and turn it into a heritage museum depicting the life of its era. The brick dairy building will also be fully restored. This deteriorated structure is one of the finest examples of its kind in the region.

Sherwood Plantation House will contain displays of its past history. Exhibits and guides will interpret the 18th- and 19th-century household as well as the plantation and farm life that transpired on this and surrounding properties over several centuries. Access to family genealogies connected with the Sherwood Plantation House and other nearby historic sites will be made available to visitors in conjunction with other cultural facilities. Oral histories related to personal experiences of living along the costal bays will be put into user-friendly formats.

Although the restoration work will be extensive and costly, the completed project will be unique in the Mid-Atlantic coastal region, if not along the entire Atlantic Coast. The attached brochure gives detailed information regarding our mission as well as a description of the work.

There are more than 25 other unique historic sites and buildings within a 10-mile radius. This represents a significant opportunity to create a linked cluster of attractions that will draw large numbers of tourists interested in the heritage of the area. Taken together, these historic sites may be placed together on the National Register of Historic Places as a tightly knit area of unprecedented local significance.

Time is of the essence due to the fact that, if the work is not started immediately, there is a significant risk of further deterioration. If this should occur, a historic treasure of tremendous prominence will have been lost forever. Over the next three years, we will require an estimated $250,000 to complete the restoration and open the doors to public admission.

To date, we have obtained funds from several sources. The State has granted us $50,000 in monies from its Historic Preservation Incentive Fund. The County Commissioners have contributed another $25,000. The Smith Preservation Fund, administered by the Walpole Foundation, has awarded us a $10,000 grant, and private contributors have given $20,000. We would be happy to meet with you at any time to discuss our request.

Sincerely,
Valerie J. Mann

Appendix F

Sample Proposal

**MAPLEWOOD, (ANY STATE) POLICE DEPARTMENT
ASSISTANCE TO RURAL LAW ENFORCEMENT TO COMBAT
CRIME AND DRUGS
APRIL 15, 2009–CATEGORY I
U.S. DEPARTMENT OF JUSTICE**

STATEMENT OF THE PROBLEM

Our project, "Community Policing in Targeted Areas," was funded by the (Any State) Governor's Office of Crime Control and Prevention from July 1, 2005 to June 30, 2008. This project has been very successful, and we wish to build on the progress made. Since funding has expired, we have started to see an increase in crime, and the citizens of the areas are feeling less secure. This funding was directed toward:

1. Purchase of two (2) additional patrol bicycles and related equipment
2. Overtime for narcotics street sweeps
3. Overtime for the crime prevention unit to give additional presentations
4. Overtime for increased patrol coverage in the downtown, the South Bay Apartment Complex, and the housing units owned by the Maplewood Housing Authority

During the first year, we made a total of 57 drug arrests. In addition, for the first year, the Crime Prevention Unit was involved in 15 programs.

A number of man-hours were involved in bicycle patrol in the Oak Street and Smith Avenue area, along with the business district. Shift supervisors commented that the extra patrols in these areas allowed them to concentrate patrols in other areas of the City and thus freed them to handle other problems. Officers and community members feel that the bicycle and foot patrols have been effective in maintaining a secure feeling among the residents.

We found that prior to the inception of this program, many citizens in these areas were reluctant to contact the police department to report crimes due to the fear of retribution from the perpetrators. Our three years of operating this program saw us steadily building our rapport with the residents of the targeted area. It is important to continue building this relationship.

We have noted that no crimes take place when we are present in the community. In one incident during the period when we were receiving state funding, officers on overtime funded by this grant observed a breaking and entering. After apprehending the suspect, we were able to tie him to three other unsolved breaking and entering cases. These crimes would not have been solved without the use of grant funds for overtime.

Input from our citizens has been invaluable in helping us to solve and prevent crimes. Information obtained from residents is often the only evidence that we have.

There remains a need for additional police presence in these areas.

It has been necessary to utilize overtime funds for this project. We are stretched very thin in other areas of the City with other problems. There has been no possibility of our being able to devote this amount of overtime to this problem using our own funds. Without Justice Department funding, the crime rate in the targeted areas will go up significantly.

The median household income for the City was $32,118 per the 2000 Census, which was only 66.3% of the state's median income of $48,421. The City also has a high percentage of persons below the poverty level. In addition to this, the City's assessable base is quite low. These factors all dictate that it is impossible to raise taxes to the extent needed to cover the cost of this program.

The unemployment rate for our county, Fairmont, was 11.2% in January of 2009 and 7.3% in January of 2008. The City's budget is totally inadequate to fund this program. Our revenues have dropped dramatically due to the sharp drop in housing starts.

It is particularly important to target the high-crime downtown, as we are working very hard to revitalize that area. In 2003, we were designated a "Revitalization Main Street Area" and have been working to reverse the decline in the downtown.

Our department is already stretched to respond to other situations in the city. The Maplewood Police Department is the third largest police department within the seven easternmost counties in the state, with only Pomona and Dale City having a greater number of officers. It shares its third place position with the Reedsville Police Department. The City of Maplewood is one of the largest municipalities in the area with a population of 10,911. The City operates one of only two municipal police departments in Fairmont County, the other being the Bethel Police Department. We are often called upon to assist outside the boundaries of the City. Fairmont County, at 983 square miles, is geographically the largest county in the state. Many of its communities are geographically isolated.

We will be able to begin this project immediately upon notification of grant award. We already have the structure in place from the previous program and have identified those areas that should receive concentrated patrol. In addition, the department has already identified the officers who are interested in working on this program. The department is aware of the various community and neighborhood activities that we should attend in the targeted areas. In essence, we will be able to pick up where we left off in a very short period of time. We expect to complete our community patrol by the end of the 24-month grant period.

This project will enhance economic benefits by providing additional income for our officers, many of whom rely upon overtime in order to stay financially viable. Due to the city's extremely adverse budgetary situation, we have not been able to provide overtime for needed projects.

PROJECT DESIGN AND IMPLEMENTATION

The Maplewood Police Department is requesting $50,000 to utilize for overtime in order to enhance patrols in high crime areas. Our project will begin on August 1, 2009 and will be completed on July 31, 2011. Approximately $25,000 will be used in each of the two program years to provide an additional 675 hours of overtime per year for a total of 1,350 hours over the course of the program. This will allow us to spend an additional 2 hours per day in these high crime areas. Overtime will be targeted for increased patrol coverage in the downtown, at the South Bay apartment complex, and at the housing units owned by the Maplewood Housing Authority:

Our goal is to reduce the level of crime in our targeted area. Objectives are as follows:

This project will satisfy the goals of the Recovery Act. The extra income obtained by these officers will be spent in our local community. At the present time, without overtime hours, our officers do not have the funds for any discretionary spending. This additional income will allow them to purchase

OBJECTIVES	OUTCOMES
Reach more citizens with crime prevention activities, and educate the public regarding ways in which they can prevent crime.	Number of crime prevention presentations; number of contacts with citizens; number of hours spent with citizens.
Increase the number of hours of patrol as compared to the present.	Number of hours of patrol.
Reduce the crime rate by 25%.	Number of crimes committed.
Increase the conviction rate by 25%.	Number and percent of convictions obtained.
Increase the feeling of comfort and security among our citizens.	Anecdotal reports from citizens on their level of satisfaction with police services.

goods and services that will support the city's businesses. These establishments have been hard hit by the recession due to the fact that our citizens have been wary of buying anything that is not absolutely essential. Grant funds for this project will help to retain our officers and infuse a significant amount of cash into the community. It is conceivable that we would have to lay off some of our officers without these funds.

Our program will meet the goals and objectives of our category by allowing a concentration of manpower to be placed in high crime areas. We have found that reductions in the crime rate and increases in the conviction rate, as well as our citizens' feelings of security, are directly related to the number of hours we patrol. We will implement our project through the following steps: (1) identification of officers to work the overtime, (2) completion of plan for areas and time frames in which this patrol will be conducted, and (3) actual patrol.

This program is significant due to the fact that it represents an opportunity to enhance the economic well-being of our community while at the same time fighting crime in high crime areas. We already know that this approach is successful, and we look forward to lowering crime even further. In rural areas, we have found that concentrated patrol in certain areas prevents crime from occurring. This program is thus significant and improves the functioning of the criminal justice system in a rural area.

We only have one program activity—overtime patrol. This is linked to our goal and all of our objectives and will be the direct stimulus for achieving the performance measures.

Our timeline is as follows:

August 1, 2009—Identify officers to be involved in this program
August 1, 2009 to August 31, 2009—Prepare plan for use of overtime
September 1, 2009 July 31, 2011—Overtime patrol takes place

The deliverables, which consist of the 1,350 overtime hours, will be achieved on a consistent basis throughout the program period. We expect to expend an approximately equal number of overtime hours per month on this project.

CAPABILITIES/COMPETENCIES

Chief William P. Darby will be responsible for oversight of this project. He will be assisted by Captain Darrell Small. The department has a great deal of experience in managing federal and state grants. We therefore already have a structure in place to track draw downs and grant expenditures separately from other federal funding. Financial record-keeping will be handled by Mr. Edward Walsh, the City's Clerk/Treasurer for the past 20 years.

We have had experience with a wide range of grant programs, including the Bulletproof Vest Partnership Program, the Local Law Enforcement Block Grant Program, the COPS Universal Hiring Program, and COPS MORE. The Cambridge CSAFE Program has become a model for other CSAFE grantees. We have seen a 13% decrease in crime in the area. Activities under this program include the operation of a substation and office in the CSAFE area, various community activities, the dedication of two officers on a full-time basis, cooperation with rental agents in the area, and various other crime prevention activities. Our program has received numerous honors and has been responsible for a significant increase in citizen contact.

IMPACT/OUTCOMES, EVALUATION, SUSTAINMENT, AND DESCRIPTION OF THE APPLICANT'S PLAN FOR THE COLLECTION OF DATA REQUIRED FOR PERFORMANCE MEASURES

We hereby certify to our willingness and capacity to participate in an evaluation to be managed by the National Institute of Justice. Our capacity may be demonstrated through our past experience in grants and sophisticated data management system.

Information regarding the performance measures shown above can all be generated through our department's regular recordkeeping. We customarily retain data on the number of hours worked, number of crimes committed, and number of convictions. Anecdotal information from our citizens will be collected by officers on patrol. We will analyze and assess this information on a quarterly basis in order to determine if project goals are being met. We will prepare a written project evaluation for each quarter and a final evaluation at the end of the project.

We will make every effort to locate either budgeted funds or other grants to sustain this project when this grant ends.

These Recovery Act Performance Measures are not applicable: job creation, partnerships, referrals to other agencies, and submissions to an intelligence database.

Appendix G

Sample Budget

OMB APPROVAL NO. 1121–0188
EXPIRES 5–98 (Rev. 1/97)

Purpose: The Budget Detail Worksheet may be used as a guide to assist you in the preparation of the budget and budget narrative. You may submit the budget and budget narrative using this form or in the format of your choice (plain sheets, your own form, or a variation of this form). However, all required information (including the budget narrative) must be provided. Any category of expense not applicable to your budget may be deleted.

A. Personnel—List each position by title and name of employee, if available. Show the annual salary rate and the percentage of time to be devoted to the project. Compensation paid for employees engaged in grant activities must be consistent with that paid for similar work within the applicant organization.

Patrol Deputy—1,500 overtime hours @ $35 = $52,500

Name/Position Computation Cost

SUB-TOTAL: $52,500

B. Fringe Benefits—Fringe benefits should be based on actual known costs or an established formula. Fringe benefits are for the personnel listed in budget category (A) and only for the percentage of time devoted to the project. Fringe benefits on overtime hours are limited to FICA, Workman's Compensation, and Unemployment Compensation.

N/A

Name/Position Computation Cost

SUB-TOTAL _____
Total Personnel & Fringe Benefits: $52,500

OJP FORM 7150/1 (5–95)

C. Travel—Itemize travel expenses of project personnel by purpose (e.g., staff to training, field interviews, advisory group meeting, etc.). Show the basis of computation (e.g., six people to 3-day training at $X airfare, $X lodging, $X subsistence). In training projects, travel and meals for trainees should be listed separately. Show the number of trainees and the unit costs involved. Identify the location of travel, if known. Indicate source of Travel Policies applied, Applicant or Federal Travel Regulations.

> To Washington, D.C., for one meeting—the other location is not known
> Transportation, 2 trips @ $110 = $220
> Hotel, 4 nights @ $150 = $600
> Meals, $85/day/deputy, 4 days for two deputies = $680
> We have utilized our own travel policies.

Purpose of Travel Location Item Computation Cost

TOTAL: $1,500

D. Equipment—List nonexpendable items that are to be purchased. Nonexpendable equipment is tangible property having a useful life of more than two years and an acquisition cost of $5,000 or more per unit. (Note: Organization's own capitalization policy may be used for items costing less than $5,000.) Expendable items should be included either in the "supplies" category or in the "Other" category. Applicants should analyze the cost benefits of purchasing versus leasing equipment, especially high-cost items and those subject to rapid technical advances. Rented or leased equipment costs should be listed in the "Contractual" category. Explain how the equipment is necessary for the success of the project. Attach a narrative describing the procurement method to be used.

N/A

Item Computation Cost

TOTAL _____

E. Supplies—List items by type (office supplies, postage, training materials, copying paper, and expendable equipment items costing less that $5,000, such as books, hand-held tape recorders) and show the basis for computation.

(Note: Organization's own capitalization policy may be used for items costing less than $5,000.) Generally, supplies include any materials that are expendable or consumed during the course of the project.

N/A

Supply Items Computation Cost

TOTAL _____

F. Construction—As a rule, construction costs are not allowable. In some cases, minor repairs or renovations may be allowable. Check with the program office before budgeting funds in this category.

N/A

Purpose Description of Work Cost

TOTAL _____

G. Consultants/Contracts—Indicate whether applicant's formal, written Procurement Policy or the Federal Acquisition Regulations are followed.

Consultant Fees: For each consultant enter the name, if known, service to be provided, hourly or daily fee (8-hour day), and estimated time on the project. Consultant fees in excess of $450 per day require additional justification and prior approval from OJP.

Name of Consultant Service Provided Computation Cost

Subtotal _____

Consultant Expenses: List all expenses to be paid from the grant to the individual consultants in addition to their fees (i.e., travel, meals, lodging, etc.).

Item Location Computation Cost

Subtotal _____

Contracts: Provide a description of the product or service to be procured by contract and an estimate of the cost. Applicants are encouraged to promote free and open competition in awarding contracts. A separate justification must be provided for sole source contracts in excess of $100,000.

N/A

Item Cost

Subtotal _____

TOTAL _____

H. Other Costs—List items (e.g., rent, reproduction, telephone, janitorial or security services, and investigative or confidential funds) by major type and the basis of the computation. For example, provide the square footage and the cost per square foot for rent, or provide a monthly rental cost and how many months to rent.

N/A

Description Computation Cost

TOTAL _____

I. Indirect Costs—Indirect costs are allowed only if the applicant has a federally approved indirect cost rate. A copy of the rate approval (a fully executed, negotiated agreement) must be attached. If the applicant does not have an approved rate, one can be requested by contacting the applicant's cognizant federal agency, which will review all documentation and approve a rate for the applicant organization, or if the applicant's accounting system permits, costs may be allocated in the direct costs categories.

Description Computation Cost

N/A
TOTAL _____

Budget Summary—When you have completed the budget worksheet, transfer the totals for each category to the spaces below. Compute the total direct costs and the total project costs. Indicate the amount of federal requested and the amount of nonfederal funds that will support the project.

Budget Category Amount

A. Personnel: $52,500
B. Fringe Benefits _____
C. Travel: $1,500
D. Equipment _____
E. Supplies _____
F. Construction _____
G. Consultants/Contracts _____
H. Other _____
Total Direct Costs $54,000
I. Indirect Costs
TOTAL PROJECT COSTS: $54,000
Federal Request: $54,000
Nonfederal Amount: 0

Appendix H

Sample Budget Narrative

SLADE COUNTY, (ANY STATE) SHERIFF'S DEPARTMENT
APRIL 17, 2009
**ASSISTANCE TO RURAL LAW ENFORCEMENT
TO COMBAT CRIME AND DRUGS OVERTIME FOR
MARINE PATROL AND ANTI-GANG ACTIVITY**

Overtime for marine patrol—750 hours @ $35 per hour = $26,250
(This overtime will be expended evenly throughout the two-year grant period)

Overtime for anti-gang efforts—750 hours @ $35 per hour = $26,250
TOTAL: $52,500
Two grant related meetings:

Meeting in Washington, D.C.—two staff members @ $375 = $750
Meeting within the region—two staff members @ $375 = $750
TOTAL: $1,500
GRAND TOTAL: $54,000

Notes: We are within driving distance of Washington, D.C., and within driving distance of any city in the region at which the second meeting could be held. We are therefore budgeting $110 per trip for transportation costs and assume that both staff members would be traveling together. We have assumed that each meeting would last two days. Our budget for meals is $85 per deputy per day, for a grand total of $680 for the two meetings. We are also allowing $150 for four nights of lodging for these two meetings.

Index

About the Author

VALERIE J. MANN is the President of Mann and Mann Grant Solutions of Fruitland, Maryland, a consulting firm that provides grant search, grant writing, and grant administration services. Ms. Mann holds a B.A. in Foreign Policy Analysis from the School of International Service at The American University in Washington, D.C., is a member of Mensa, and was honored as an Outstanding Young Woman of America.